wordeee

A
BLESSING

Women of Color Teaming Up to
LEAD, EMPOWER AND THRIVE

BONITA C. STEWART AND
JACQUELINE ADAMS

Foreword by
Kenneth Chenault, Chairman and Managing Director of General Catalyst,
Former Chairman and CEO of American Express

wordeee
where words connect

A
BLESSING

Women of Color Teaming Up to
LEAD, EMPOWER AND THRIVE

First edition October 2020

ISBN-13: 978-1-946274-45-8 (Paperback)
        978-1-946274-46-5 (ebook)
        978-1-946274-47-2 (Hardcover)

Library of Congress Control Number: 2020936645

Photography by Damani Moyd

Makeup by Danielle Waugh, InHerBeautyNY

Jacket design by Omomato

Interior Design by Amit Dey

Website by Fusion Second

Published by Wordeee in the United States, Beacon, New York 2020

Website: www.wordeee.com
Twitter
Facebook
e-mail: contact@wordeee.com

Advance Praise

"Stewart's and Adams' insights are a blueprint for surrounding yourself with success by embracing the enormous power of the blessing to prosper and create an atmosphere of abundance, influence and well-being."

—Gina Stikes,
VP Corporate Communications, Quibi

"It is indeed a blessing to have Bonita and Jackie share their stories that serve as beacons to women of color."

—Ann M. Fudge,
Former Chairman & CEO, Young & Rubicam Brands

"A long overdue playbook for teamwork among women of color by two savvy HBS alums who have shattered the glass ceiling."

—Henry McGee,
*Senior Lecturer, Harvard Business School and
Retired President of HBO Home Entertainment*

"Bonita Stewart and Jacqueline Adams have answered the call to Black women everywhere to team up and use our special skills, strengths and experiences to take our seat at the table. The knowledge and research in this book provide the blueprint for personal and professional growth designed to create change and success for generations of blessings to come.

—Cheryl Mayberry McKissack,
President and Co-Owner,
Black Opal and Fashion Fair Cosmetics

"*A Blessing* is a book by people and about people who are simultaneously the rarest and most abundant among us. They represent our heart and soul and a definitive piece of the solution to a more fulfilled humanity. I whole heartedly recommend that this become required reading for anyone who wants to have true, long lasting impact in the world."

—Jacques-Philippe Piverger,
Co-founder, Ozone Ventures

"Harnessing the power of inclusive ambition is paramount for companies to thrive in this decade. *A Blessing* opens up a new dialogue around the importance of allies and sisterhood."

—Stacy Brown-Philpot,
CEO, TaskRabbit

Dedication

To our ancestors, generations of mothers and fathers whose strength and courage enabled us to thrive, and to future generations of leaders of color to whom we pass the baton.

Table of Contents

Preface

by

*Debra L. Lee, Chairman and CEO Emeritus,
BET Networks, Board Member of Marriott Int'l,
Burberry Group PLC and AT&T Inc., and Chair,
Leading Women Defined Foundation*

As a Black female CEO, I have often been called a unicorn in the boardrooms and corporate offices which I frequent. I have always known that Black women are special. I have hired, worked with and managed them. I have mentored them, convened them and cheered them on in their careers. But I have never heard them referred to as Blessings—until now. The moment I realized that a group of unicorns is called a blessing, I thought how perfect and powerful a title it is: *A Blessing: Women of Color Teaming Up to Lead, Empower and Thrive.*

This book by Bonita Stewart and Jackie Adams shines a light on the qualities which women of color executives bring to any company and how, when we team up and support each other, we can accomplish so much and thrive.

With their proprietary research, the authors prove the case that we women of color are natural leaders, and we excel in accomplishing any and every goal. I hope companies read this book and that it causes a shift in thinking that diversity and inclusion are not only the right things to do. They are GREAT for business.

Foreword

by

Kenneth Chenault, Chairman and Managing Director
of General Catalyst, Former Chairman
and CEO of American Express

T hroughout my career, I have paraphrased a quote from Napoleon: "The role of a leader is to define reality and to give hope." Jacqueline Adams and Bonita Stewart have written a book that accomplishes both for women of color and their allies in the business world.

While Jackie's and Bonita's book is focused on business, it does so through the lens of middle–class childhoods, unapologetically Black perspectives, and with an unflinching analysis of this country's history of racism — yet with an optimism about the future that I recognized immediately as echoing my own. Leadership and collaboration are important themes that run deeply throughout the book, which many have described as FBF (fresh, bold, and fierce). I couldn't agree more.

As an undergraduate at Bowdoin College, I studied the careers of early African American students who came before me. Of the ~20 Black men who graduated between 1910 and 1950, half earned grades high enough to be admitted to the prestigious Phi Beta Kappa Society and yet half were not allowed to live on campus because of their race. Their attempts to have the career that I did were thwarted by Jim Crow practices and blatant racism that still permeate far too much of American society today.

From post–slavery reconstruction to the early 1900s through Brown v. Board of Education, there has been a tremendous gap in opportunity. If we had been granted the same basic equal human rights after Emancipation, think about what a different place we'd all be in as African Americans and as a society overall. We've always had the brainpower, the grit and the resilience to succeed. Instead, so much potential has been wasted.

Often, I am asked why progress has been so slow on racial diversity in business in particular. I believe that a real commitment is required from business leaders and society driven by the basic belief that it is not enough for human beings to be simply tolerated or accepted. To truly make progress, African Americans, women, and other historically marginalized people must feel that they are a part of society. And for that to happen, they must not be just accepted; they must be embraced.

Further, I fundamentally believe that corporations exist because society allows them to exist. Therefore, all business-es have an obligation to contribute positively to the better-ment and progress of society. Representation matters. It should come as no surprise that by placing people of diverse backgrounds, race and gender in positions of power, with time, the fabric of leadership begins to change. I've seen that change, which is powerful and compelling. And I'm proud of having driven some of that change throughout my career.

However, diversity and inclusion have not been widely adopted in the technology and venture capital industries, and that is in large part why I have chosen to focus this next chapter of my career in these areas. It's ironic that technology has improved our society in so many ways, and yet the leadership of the industry remains largely unchanged, but not forever.

As Bonita's and Jackie's research and interviews illustrate, this next generation of professionals, in particular young women of color, are appropriately and deservedly demanding equity. They know their value, as do the executives with the power to hire them. And, as the book illustrates, when women early in their careers collaborate with women with established careers, their collective knowledge and power are absolutely unstoppable. Bonita and Jackie leave us with an important call to action: becoming and empowering true allies committed to greeting, welcoming and embracing women of color into centers of power. Ultimately, the disruptors will have to innovate beyond themselves to truly change the world.

A Word from the Authors

Women of Color in Business:
Cross Generational Survey©

As we began to conceptualize this book, we found massive amounts of data about women of color and women at work. We were inspired by and even participated in the groundbreaking, in–depth research that Harvard Business School scholars conducted about Black men and women alumni: *Spheres of Influence: A Portrait of Black MBA Program Alumni.*

We were surprised, however, that we could not find surveys that compared and contrasted the different generations of women of color at work. Such research may exist or may be in the process of being conducted, but it wasn't immediately apparent. Therefore, we conducted our own. We named our research the *Women of Color in Business: Cross Generational Survey©.*

In business, relationships matter. Jackie met Scott Siff, co–founder of Quadrant Strategies, more than a decade ago

1

and together, Scott and Jackie have collaborated on a series of non–profit activities. Jackie had long admired Scott's work as a pollster for major corporations and influential politicians. She was happy to introduce Scott and his team to Bonita.

Together, we refined a series of topics tied to the themes we anticipated for this book. Within weeks, we had data from 4,005 Black, LatinX, Asian and white "desk" or knowledge workers across four generations: Boomers (ages 55–72); Gen X (ages 38–54); Millennials (ages 23–37); and Gen Z (ages 16–22).

Our list of about 13 topics grew into 91 questions. The survey was fielded over less than a month, online, in the fall of 2019. Granted, we oversampled African American and LatinX women, but we felt the experiences of Asian and white women were important controls. Full details about our methodology can be found in our Endnotes. An executive summary can be found on our website, www.leadempowerthrive.com.[1]

We were heartened by the raw data that came back as well as the reactions of Scott's colleagues, Hannah Leverson and Mary Amis. The Quadrant Strategies team helped us generate the first versions of the Word Clouds and infographics used throughout this work.

Some of the results are inspiring, some predictable. However, all are important for current and future employers. We sought advice for achieving success for women of color in the workplace from all of the races. You can find those Word Clouds in Chapter Four.

As a teaser for the full survey, we want you to take a close look at the advice we separated out, advice offered by our 1,604 African American women by generation.

Black Women Say— "Never Give Up"

The most often stated answers of our Black women respondents are the largest, boldest font size, but study the variety of sizes of other answers as well.

Given our history of struggle, it was reassuring, albeit predictable, to see that the most consistent and loudest message was: "Never Give Up." Most of the African American women also said: "Work Hard" and "Don't Let Others Stop You." The troubling but realistic implication is somebody might try to stop you. And of course, many have. But Black women also said, "Keep pushing!" Across the generations, many said: "Don't Let Color Define You."

When we took a closer look at the women's responses, there were intriguing differences between the four generations.

Black Boomer women (Bonita's and Jackie's generation— ages 55–72) sounded like mothers and grandmothers. Much of the burden of the advice for success was self–directed:

- Get an education
- Know your worth
- Be professional
- Do your job
- Listen and learn
- Put God first
- You can achieve
- Stay focused
- Be confident
- Believe in yourself

Black Boomer Women

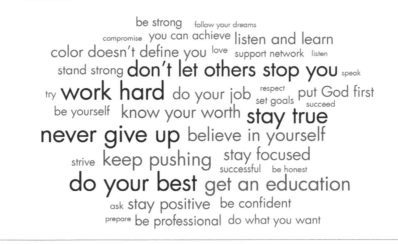

Women of Color in Business: Cross Generational Survey©

The Black Gen X women (ages 38–54) were a bit more defiant:

- Don't be afraid
- Just do you
- Don't change for anyone

Black GenX Women

keep going
you're beautiful focus be resilient believe
color doesn't define you just do you
push be strong do your best listen keep your head up
don't let others stop you achieve
keep pushing always do your best
love don't be afraid work hard
never stop stay strong
others don't define you prove people wrong
you can do anything never give up
be confident don't change for anyone
do what you want

Women of Color in Business: Cross Generational Survey©

4

The Black Millennials (ages 23–37) were both self–focused and defiant:

- Always do your best
- Believe in yourself
- Don't be discouraged
- Don't be afraid
- Do what you want
- Just be yourself

Black Millennials Women

ask   learn
don't be discouraged
be better work harder stay strong
try work hard meet your goals deserve
stay true to yourself believe in yourself be professional
do what you want   always do your best
career   focus   strive   God first   love   greatness
never give up stay focused know your worth
stand up   keep your head up do your job do your best
just be yourself color doesn't define you be authentic
don't let others stop you keep going
                                   be confident
don't be afraid keep pushing
don't settle positivity

Women of Color in Business: Cross Generational Survey©

Happily, the Black Gen Z population, still in high school and college (ages 16–22), was the most confident and optimistic:

- Just be yourself
- Ignore negativity
- You can do anything
- You are beautiful

Black GenZ Women

worth never stop

focus do what you want love yourself

you are beautiful just be yourself listen

keep your head up stay true do your best push

don't let others stop you follow your dreams

stay focused remember your worth believe be happy

achieve stay strong you can do anything don't stop

never give up keep pushing

don't change put yourself first ignore negativity

color doesn't define you continue no matter what

strive always do your best be confident

never give up work hard

keep going

Women of Color in Business: Cross Generational Survey©

These answers should serve as a wakeup call for current and future leaders. To be most effective going forward, exceptional leaders must understand the generational nuances within ethnic groups. Let's call this concept GD–Generational Diversity.

You read it here first.

Introduction

A group of unicorns is called a "blessing." Myth has it that seeing a unicorn brings good luck and fortune to the observer. We embrace this metaphor.

We are a blessing of Black unicorns, accomplished female leaders of color — rare yet highly visible — unmistakably increasing in number with the potential to wield significant influence around the world. The dictionary defines a blessing as "a prayer," "a stroke of luck" and "a seal of approval."

Look around. Imagine yourself as the only one, the sole sister in the business world: in a boardroom, in the C-suite, on a private jet, in any strategic planning meeting. Then imagine these Black unicorns as a collective of experience, succeeding, full of resilience, pioneering spirit and glory. Imagine, with us, a future in which a blessing of Black unicorns is empowered to team up, a future in which teaming up can fulfill our economic promise and be an act of salvation for our world.

Our work, *A Blessing: Women of Color Teaming Up to Lead, Empower and Thrive,* presents a scholarly review of data that supports our premise for the empowerment of and collaboration by Black women in business. This book also includes the results of our original, proprietary research, our *Women of Color in Business: Cross Generational Survey©* which examined the views of 4,005 female "desk" or "knowledge workers" across four races (Black, LatinX, Asian and white) and four generations (Gen Z, Millennials, Gen X and Boomers). In addition, we interviewed several successful Harvard Business School alumnae of color, across three of the four generations, whose observations and lived experiences amplify our themes.

Our work is reflective, filled with personal anecdotes and experiences, and offers real–life lessons and actions steps through what we call our Living Log. First and foremost, though, we put forth a theory and a call to action for Black women to come together—along with our allies of all colors—for the greater good.

In our historical context, women of color have had limited or no power. We've been victims of racism and misogyny, victims of the divide and rule and the divide and conquer strategies of slave owners and overseers. We have been separated from our families, separated along color lines for hot, back–breaking jobs in the "field" versus those inside in the kitchens and nurseries of the "house" and by society in general.

> ***Divide and rule*** *(from Latin divide et impera), or **divide and conquer**, in politics and sociology is gaining and maintaining power by breaking up larger concentrations of power into pieces that individually have less power than the one implementing the strategy.²*

When slavery ended, the separations didn't. Psychologically separated from our true identity, we carried over ideals of "white is right" for years. Inter–ethnic separation along color lines left over from insidious mental programming led to, for example, the "paper bag" test, too often a deciding factor for which social organizations, colleges, fraternities and sororities to which we could be considered for admittance. The lighter the better, but no one whose skin was darker than a brown paper bag was allowed.

Along with the perceived benefits of good hair, we developed a crabs in a barrel syndrome further promoted by the notion of a Talented Tenth, which created delusional comfort for the few who succeeded in getting to the top. Ironically, the perceived physical benefits of shade and hair texture were the results of generations of our grandmothers and great–grandmothers being routinely raped by their owners, producing additional capital, i.e. additional children or assets for those owners. If we're honest, admiration for hair and skin tones was a manifestation of self–loathing for our original blackness.

Fast forward to the 21st century, and we are in a totally new world, in different career environments. Through advances in technology, racial and gender awareness is exploding at a rapid pace. As women, we are now being told to "lean in," to assert ourselves at work and at home and grab success. For women of color, however, we have the additional burden of often being the only one. Leaning in means we have to learn how to ignore and move past our "only–ness," our soleness and our loneliness with style and confidence, to become leaders who have the skills to teach upcoming leaders the power of unity.

Let's Sit On Our Sofa

We have been there. Our invitation to sit on our sofa is what happens when you bring together a renowned network news correspondent and a seasoned tech executive who want to share what we have learned and experienced with passion and compassion.

We first met through the Harvard Business School (HBS) alumni network. For us, attending HBS was a life–altering experience that created a launching pad for our career successes and financial fulfillment, just as it has for so many global business luminaries. Over the years, we have shared in and cheered on each other's successes. After participating in the 50th anniversary celebration of the HBS African American Student Union (AASU), we felt a deep urge to do more with the insights we have gained. After all, in 1968, AASU was created by five African–American students to "enrich the ranks of Black business leadership." Indeed, the mission of HBS is to create "leaders who make a difference in the world." We want to embody, to breathe life into those missions today and for the future.

A source of inspiration for us is Lillian Lincoln Lambert, the epitome of a line from a Maya Angelou's poem, "We are the miraculous." In 1969, Lillian became the first African American woman to earn an MBA from Harvard Business School. For two lonely years, she was the only, the sole Black woman within the school's hallowed halls.

Still, she succeeded in earning her degree and built a thriving business. Since then, almost 700 smart and ambitious African American women have followed in Lillian's footsteps, many ascending to become great leaders despite their "only–ness."

Like Lillian, both of us have always felt like unicorns, as sole sisters, as raisins in our various professional bread puddings. We didn't look like the vast majority of men and women against whom we competed and with whom we collaborated throughout our business lives. Our singular and collective story has not been fully told and our pay–it–forward instincts were unfulfilled.

We consider this our time to scale Black talent, to team up, to unify with our peers to create a new center of gravity. Think of the possibilities of "sisters as a service." After all, today, we have software as a service (SaaS), a software distribution model that allows a provider to host applications and make them available to customers over the Internet, thus creating exponential scale. We propose using this same model in our unique context to scale the power of Black unity. The power of women supporting each other in the workplace and beyond is not to be underestimated.

Why Now? Let's Review the Data–Theirs and Ours.

Our work is supported by data. Before we delve into our full narrative, let's review some of the data we reference and share some of the data we collected. Data informs this work. We want you to keep the data top of mind as you read.

Demographics and Fertility

Current projections are that women of color will be in the majority in the United States by 2060, if not before. According to a 2018 *New York Times* op–ed by Charles M. Blow, both the Census Bureau and the Brookings Institution have noted the shrinking fertility rates of white women in the U.S. Blow cites this factor as one possible source of the current "white extinction anxiety."[3]

Our Ambitions

To assess women's attitudes and experiences around work and the future, we commissioned our *Women of Color in Business: Cross Generational Survey©*. Seeded throughout our various chapters, our results may be the first time Black female Boomers, Gen Xers, Millennials, and Gen Zers, all "desk workers," have been queried. For fairness and comparison purposes, we also questioned LatinX, Asian and white women. We asked about satisfaction at work and in life, stress, sources of support and inspiration, the impact of their fathers and more. In many cases, our findings dovetail with those of other surveys that we have assessed.

Overall, despite the extra scrutiny Black and brown women face in the hiring process and on the job, we are the most optimistic and confident about the future. We are leaving traditional corporations in favor of our own entrepreneurial ventures in striking numbers. We are trendsetters, and we know it. But we are open to working with allies of other races, metaphorical doormen, who can and should accept and usher us into the realms of power for which we are more than qualified to enter.

Our Impact on the Overall Economy

Dr. Cindy Pace, global chief diversity and inclusion officer for MetLife, quantified the impact of Black women on the economy in the August 2018 *Harvard Business Review*: "$1 trillion as consumers and $361 billion in revenue as entrepreneurs, launching companies at 4x the rate of all women–owned businesses."[4]

This means women of color are a force in the U.S. economy. Teaming up, indeed, could literally be an act of economic salvation.

The C–Suite

Dr. Pace's research confirmed what we, scholars and think tanks have found: Women of color in the workplace are undeniably ambitious. We want power and influence. We confidently seize opportunities. We pursue management challenges. We cultivate influential mentors. And yet, "Black women's advancement into leadership roles has remained stagnant, even as the number of them in professional and managerial roles has increased."

In late 2014, *Harvard Business Review* anticipated Dr. Pace's findings and reported Black women are nearly three times more likely than white to aspire for a position of power with a prestigious title. And yet, white women are about twice as likely as Black women to attain one. More research shows diverse leadership benefits companies in all sectors. Firms with the most ethnically diverse executive teams were 33% more likely to outperform their peers on profitability. Those with executive–level gender diversity worldwide had a 21% likelihood of outperforming their industry competitors. But these realizations have not yet created lasting change. In fact, there has been backsliding.[5] Only a handful of women of color have ever been CEOs of Fortune 500 companies. However, currently, Ursula Burns at Xerox, Ann Fudge at Y&R Brands, Indra Nooyi at PepsiCo and Geisha Williams at PG&E have all moved on from their CEO jobs. In their May 2020 ranking of the Fortune 500, editors announced that 36 women were CEOs of the largest companies, an increase over 2019's 33. Three of these women were of color, Sonia Syngal at The Gap, Advanced Micro Devices CEO Lisa Su and Yum China CEO Joey Wat. However, editors noted that no Black women or Latinas run Fortune 500 companies. In 2019, Mary Winston, then interim CEO of Bed Bath & Beyond, was the first Black CEO since Ursula Burns but one year later, she did not make the list.[6]

According to the search firm Korn Ferry, the dearth of senior Black leaders in corporate America is the result of "high potential African American leadership talent" … "choosing to opt out of corporate life for independent careers." The reasons: "Lack of representation in the C–suite and boardroom, conscious and unconscious biases, and lack of career support. This finding poses and increases the risk for organizations recruiting and trying to retain future African American executives and leaders."

The Korn Ferry findings are buttressed by a study by LeanIn. org with McKinsey, released in late October 2018. Forty–five percent of women of color reported being the only person of their race in work situations. Sadly, the study also found that our "sole–ness," being "the only one" has profound costs, especially on a team, in the C–suite or on a project.

- The LeanIn.org/McKinsey study found that women who spend time as "the only" are one–and–a–half times more likely to think about leaving their jobs than women who work with other women.
- Eighty percent of women in the "only" category, compared to two–thirds of women across the board, say they have experienced micro–aggressions, from being mistaken for someone more junior to needing to provide more evidence of their competence.
- Women who are onlys also report being sexually harassed at higher numbers.[7]

To solve these problems, Lean In and McKinsey recommend that companies hire and promote more women. That's been the traditional response. And of course, companies should hire and promote more women. But as Korn Ferry found, there's a Catch–22. Without more and more visible people of color at the top, younger people of color, those beginning their careers, are opting out. One of our HBS alumnae, a senior executive at LinkedIn, Jacqueline Jones, has put it bluntly, "You can't be what you can't see."[8]

Entrepreneurs

According to the 2018 State of Women–Owned Business Report commissioned by American Express, while the number of women–owned businesses grew by an impressive 58% from 2007 to 2018, the number of firms owned by Black women grew by a stunning 164%. There were 2.4 million African

American women–owned businesses in 2018, most owned by women in the 35 to 54 age range.[9] Black women are the only racial or ethnic group with more business ownership than their male peers, according to the Federal Reserve.[10]

Given the coming demographic surge and the economic power of women of color, something has to give. If fully engaged as a group, unicorns of color could transform capitalism. What a blessing! This book is a call for that collective.

Why Us?

Neither of us thought the world needed another book filled with self–congratulatory tales of triumph over adversity or diversity in the corporate world. However, we appreciate what we have achieved, alone and together, and we have a passion for three outcomes:

- sharing and leveraging what we've learned in our careers as a springboard for the next generation of Black leaders;
- ensuring that our personal victories are known by more than our circle of friends; and
- that we can leave a legacy that will endure and spread our message of unity.

Yes, we both have had exciting careers. Bonita was the first African-American female vice president at Google, and Jackie was the first African American female correspondent formally assigned to cover the Ronald Reagan and George H. W. Bush White Houses for CBS News. We are used to not taking no for an answer. We are used to wielding our only-ness and cultural invisibility as a cloak or a shield. We are comfortable being in command, being leaders. We have the entrepreneurial instinct.

Also, we share another, more personal bond. We are both daughters of men who loved us dearly and championed our earliest academic achievements. Sadly, both of our fathers passed away from heart disease while we were in college. Both men were so young, just 47 years old. In some respects, each of us has been achieving for two—ourselves and our fathers: smart, insightful men who matured during the Jim Crow era and, miraculously, were optimistic about their daughters' chances of success.

We were among the first beneficiaries of the groundbreaking opportunities the Civil Rights and Women's Rights movements pried open in the late 1960s and the 1970s. Armed with our families' support, our personal drive and our HBS degrees, we were well prepared to grab hold of and properly execute those opportunities.

Indeed, the HBS African American alumni network first brought us together. Jackie earned her MBA in 1978 and Bonita in 1983. We are both among the alumnae profiled for the school's twin celebrations of half a century of women in the MBA program and the founding of the African American Student Union.[11]

Although we were several years apart in graduate school, teaming up is a deliberate component of the HBS African American alumni experience, and we are proud to embody it.

Over the decades, we have mentored and supported one another, primarily in an ad hoc fashion. But we have long recognized what the research is now confirming: There is toxicity in the aloneness, the "only–ness," which accomplished women of color typically experience. And there are antidotes.

We want to explore the reasons for that toxicity and its career limitations, how we have experienced them and how this toxicity is hurting the very organizations for which we work. But we also want to offer strategies for thriving and making the tough calls. We want to provide ways of celebrating our possibilities together. We want to demonstrate specifically how and why, as poet Maya Angelou wrote and Lillian Lincoln Lambert first lived, "we are the miraculous."

Perhaps our zeal is inherited. Bonita's paternal grandfather was described in the *History of the American Negro South Carolina* edition: "He feels the future progress of the race depends on education and unity."[12] We are making tremendous strides in education. Next up–unity.

More Than a Book, a Platform

Instead of challenging women all over the world with the will to lead, *A Blessing: Women of Color Teaming Up to Lead, Thrive and Empower* is designed to provide tools and inspiration for women of color of all generations to challenge their "only–ness."

Our book is targeted at two specific audiences:

- accomplished women of color, women in the corporate world as well as women entrepreneurs, the fastest–growing group of business leaders of color
- and our allies, wherever they may be and whatever their race.

We will give you the latest research. After all, as Harvard Business School alumnae, we know that metrics matter. But we also plan to look deeper into our hearts and souls, to examine the ways we and our "sisters" have survived over history. In their new book, *Race, Work, and Leadership*, authors/scholars Laura Morgan Roberts, Anthony J. Mayo and David A. Thomas call these personal stories "phenomenological studies: the lived experience."[13]

We will acknowledge the roles our white male allies and mentors have played in many of our successes to date, and we will offer them tips for working even more successfully with us. Most importantly, we will offer a playbook and a framework for women of color to work together, team up and shed the cloak of invisibility and aloneness.

We will provide platforms across various media to engage with each other at scale. We also have launched our website, www.LeadEmpowerThrive.com, where you can download the executive summary of our original proprietary research, *Women of Color in Business: Cross Generational Survey©*.

Following her passing at age 88, we were reminded of the inspiring words of seer and author Toni Morrison. She seemed to anticipate our efforts in the November 2003 issue of *O, The Oprah Magazine*. "I tell my students, 'When you get these jobs you have been so brilliantly trained for, just remember your real job is to free somebody else, as you have become free. If you have some power, then your job is to empower somebody else. This is not just a grab bag candy game."[14]

With today's ability to harness talent and scale our advice, our plan is to heed Ms. Morrison's challenge, to be free and to help free others, to make a difference for everyone. We welcome the dialogue as we journey together. Join the movement and create the blessing that we all rightfully deserve.

Chapter One

Our Natural Grit

Bonita Coleman Stewart's happiest day at work was when a second Black vice president, this time a man, was named within Google's business organization.

Earning her VP title in 2011 had been surreal, a significant accomplishment in the flat, hierarchical world of technology. The title symbolized passing through the golden door of opportunity, entering an inner circle, tasting the sacred water. But there was a double sense of pride and responsibility for Bonita. During the Great Recession, she was also the first and only woman chosen to lead a large U.S. revenue sector.

Bonita deserved the promotion, of course. She was successfully running a multi–billion–dollar U.S. media sales division at Google across finance, media/entertainment, automotive, and travel, managing a team of 200+ and more than 600+ clients in a hyper–growth environment.

Her three decades of leading large teams, innovating digital solutions and driving profits in major corporations in the IT, automotive and now technology fields had been recognized both inside and outside Google. But she considered it a personal triumph when another Black executive joined her.

Both her and his full regalia of experience, results and credentials said to Google employees and the business world at large that "we"–collective Black executives–can do this.

Jacqueline Adams' happiest day at work was in 1979. Introducing one of her first stories on the *CBS Evening News*, anchor Walter Cronkite, dubbed "the most trusted man in America," announced she had studied agribusiness while she earned her MBA from Harvard Business School.

Cronkite's announcing the impressive credential to America seemed to rankle some of her less well educated colleagues. Several white male correspondents made sure she knew how upset they were that the anchor had singled out her background. But for Jackie, Cronkite's decision to note her education and validate her expertise was a clear statement to the viewing audience, and to CBS News writ large, that she was qualified and wasn't just an affirmative action hire.

In hindsight, neither of us saw ourselves as "unicorns," rare and highly valuable beings in the business world. We didn't fully appreciate that being ambitious, unafraid, successful women of color made us pioneers.

We couldn't have known that decades later, Harvard Business School researchers would interview us as part of their study of our successes and those of other Black alums, both male and female. The researchers concluded that "perseverance was deemed essential to both forge new opportunities (self–employment, entrepreneurship) and confront the systemic bias in business and society. Our interviews with senior Black women pointed to resilience as an essential ingredient in their path to the executive level."[15]

Hmmm. We can appreciate the researchers' conclusions, but for us, we were just putting one foot in front of the

22

other, living out our dreams and experiencing the successes that generations of women of any color had and have been denied. At the root of our shared experience was our grit, perseverance and resilience, but also our families, our Ivy League educations and our coming into maturity at a singular moment in history, when the first few doors of opportunity began to open thanks to the Civil Rights and Women's Rights movements.

The world noticed our accomplishments long before the HBS researchers did. CBS News ran a full-page print ad in the summer of 1980. "Big Night. Big Team" touted the list of CBS correspondents and commentators assigned to cover the Republican Convention that selected Ronald Reagan as the GOP's presidential candidate. There were several other women on the team; Diane Sawyer, Susan Spencer and Lesley Stahl. There were two men of color: Ed Bradley and Lem Tucker. But Jacqueline Adams stood out as the sole woman of color and the youngest on the team at just 30 years old. Because the correspondents were listed alphabetically, her name and photo were just below those of anchor Walter Cronkite.

Bonita Stewart was singled out as a "web star" when Chrysler won the 2005 Interactive Marketer of the Year award and she was featured in an annual *Ad Age* cover story. Then Director of Interactive Communications at Chrysler, Bonita was cited for increasing sales as a result of adding a search feature on the automaker's brands website.[16]

One year later, Google came calling. Though Bonita had experienced a few stumbles in the largely male, largely white automotive hierarchy, she had gritted her teeth, learned what she needed to know about the auto industry and earned respect inside and outside Chrysler. As a result,

Google chose her to lead its automotive practice and bring digital transformation to its rapidly expanding company. Bonita was the embodiment of genuine progress: An African American woman was chosen, not the traditional white male. For her, it was sheer joy.

We may have defied the odds, but sadly, objectively, conditions have not gotten much better for women or business leaders of color in the four plus decades since we started our careers.

Today, the World Economic Forum estimates gender equality is still 99.5 years away. Plus, a quick Google search will turn up any number of articles with advice for women on leveling the playing field.[17]

Dr. Alice Eagly, a Northwestern University professor and expert on gender and leadership, recently stated that her studies show women are more likely than men to possess the leadership qualities associated with success. Women are more transformational than men. They care more about developing their followers; they listen to them and stimulate them to think "outside the box;" they are more inspirational; and they are more ethical.[18]

The natural grit of women, especially women of color, is not a secret. In the fall of 2019, we conducted our *Women of Color in Business: Cross Generational Survey*© and asked 4,005 American desk or knowledge workers a series of questions that confirmed our "unicorn" status. Our findings and our methodology can be found in the executive eummary on our website, www.leadempowerthrive.com.

Surveying four generations (Gen Z–ages 16–22, Millennials–ages 23–37, Gen X–ages 38–54 and Boomers–ages 55–72) of Black, LatinX, Asian and white women, we found that nearly half of Black women are frequently or always the only person of color in a professional situation. By contrast, 73% of white women say they rarely are "onlys." A quarter of Black women say people do not root for them at work, compared to just 15% of whites.

UNICORN STATUS AND ADDED CHALLENGES

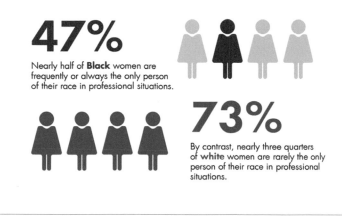

47%
Nearly half of **Black** women are frequently or always the only person of their race in professional situations.

73%
By contrast, nearly three quarters of **white** women are rarely the only person of their race in professional situations.

Women of Color in Business: Cross Generational Survey©

And yet, we women of color persist. Multiple studies have found that "Black women are nearly three times more likely than white to aspire to a position of power, with a prestigious title. However, white women are about twice as likely as Black women to attain one."[19]

The most recent U. S. Census data shows 64% of working Black women held white–collar jobs compared to 72% of all women.[20] Yet–surprise! McKinsey's 2018 study on *Women in the Workplace* found that hiring and promotion practices still favor white men. Thirty-six percent of entry–level employees and almost 70% in the C–suite are white men. For white women, a similar percentage, 31%, are entry–level employees, but the percentage shrinks dramatically for the C–suite, just 19%. For women of color: 17% entry and only 4% C–suite.[21]

The familiar term "glass ceiling" has evolved. California Senator Kamala Harris, for one, is now pledging to "break things."

In hindsight, Bonita and Jackie managed to break a lot of things. If (or when) we noticed we were "the only," a sole sister in any endeavor or location, we plowed ahead anyway, undaunted. Failure was not an option. We didn't know it, but both of us were demonstrating qualities now studied and actively taught as components of "character education." University of Pennsylvania professor Angela Duckworth has written extensively about "grit." It's the name of her 2016 book, *Grit: The Power of Passion and Perseverance.* In a nutshell, the thesis is "No whining. No complaining. No -excuses."[22]

Duckworth has written, "...there are no shortcuts to excellence. Developing real expertise, figuring out really hard problems, it all takes time—longer than most people imagine. You've got to apply those skills and produce goods or services that are valuable to people...Grit is about working on something you care about so much that you're willing to stay loyal to it...it's doing what you love, but not just falling in love—staying in love."

Duckworth's work dovetails with the research of Dr. Martin Seligman (University of Pennsylvania) and Dr. Chris Peterson (University of Michigan) that identifies 24 character strengths as leading to engaged, meaningful and purposeful lives. The nationwide KIPP Charter Schools (on whose New York City board of trustees Jackie served for a decade) has partnered with the researchers to develop a curriculum for

26

teachers, parents and students around seven of the original 24 key character components:

> Grit–perseverance and passion;
> Zest–vitality, excitement and energy;
> Self–control–the capacity to regulate thoughts, feelings and behaviors;
> Social Intelligence–an awareness of others' motives and feelings;
> Curiosity–the search for information for its own sake;
> Optimism–an expectation that the future holds positive possibilities; and
> Gratitude–appreciation for the benefits we receive from others and the desire to reciprocate.[23]

Author Paul Tough chronicled the early character education efforts at the KIPP Charter Schools in NYC and has written movingly about both the importance and impact of this work. When asked about the impact of these character markers as predictors of success, Tough has said: "Cognitive skill and IQ make a big difference; vocabulary matters. But the scientists, economists and neuroscientists and psychologists who I've been studying and writing about are really challenging the idea that IQ, that standardized test scores, that those are the most important things in a child's success. I think there's lots of evidence out there now that says that these other strengths, these character strengths, these non–cognitive skills, are at least as important in a child's success and quite possibly more important."[24]

Years before these character components were identified and studied, these profound markers of success have shown up at every stage of our lives.

Bonita's Story—Most Likely to Succeed

I started off as an "only" an only girl. I was born with grit, what I call quiet ambition. My mother said I struggled with an umbilical cord wrapped around my neck. Nonetheless, I made it through. She said that was why I always kept my head peering high and looking beyond.

My greatgrandfather, George Washington Coleman, or "Wash," was of Irish extraction and was shown as "Mulatto" on the 1870 Federal Census for South Carolina. Wash was considered quite prosperous by the standards of the day. His obituary, printed in a local Aiken, South Carolina, newspaper, indicated he had accumulated "quite a nice home." He was obviously committed to land ownership for when he died, county court records indicated he owned approximately 2,800 acres of land. According to other documents, at some point in his life, he owned as many as 3600 acres of land. In addition to farming, Wash Coleman was also a brick mason. Family oral accounts and obituary records indicate that, upon his death, he left each of his children a home. Also, Coleman Thankful Baptist Church was named in his honor. His son, my grandfather, John W. Coleman, was a well-known builder of churches and pastor of Majority Baptist Church in Spartanburg, South Carolina. A graduate of the historically black Benedict College in Columbia, South Carolina, he also served as a trustee of Morris College in Sumpter, South Carolina, another historically black college with Baptist origins.[25]

My father, Major John W. Coleman, Jr., chose a different, more unlikely profession. He was a pioneer, a pilot in the U.S. Air Force, an officer and one of only two African American pilots who flew the world's first supersonic bomber. Though he was a product of the South, you never would have known he ever lived there. He had perfect elocution and carried himself with a noble air. In high school, he was known as "the crooner." You were either in awe or standing at attention.

My mother left North Carolina A & T University in her senior year to marry her hometown sweetheart. She decided being a stay–at–home wife and mother was the better option. With my two brothers, we led a wholesome life, not a wealthy life. I always considered it a Leave It to Beaver *life, for those who remember the television show. This sitcom defines the "golly gee" respectability of the 1950s and '60s, where dad Ward Cleaver always gets home in time for dinner; mom June cleans the house wearing a dress and pearls; and kids Wally and the Beav always learn a lesson by the end of the episode.*[26]

As a youngster, I was focused on achievement. I did extremely well in school, earned extra cash for good grades and always attained honor roll status. I built a financial stockpile for loans to my brothers (with interest, of course). In retrospect, these were my formative years on my path to becoming a leader.

I've been working since my teens, from odd babysitting jobs to fast food restaurants to fashion boutiques. While I am blessed with parents who owned their home and provided me with everything (food, shelter, safety – everything based on Maslow's hierarchy of needs), in my soul, I longed for financial independence. I saw life as a ladder; You keep climbing and at each rung, you give it your absolute best.

My penchant for achievement must have shone through when my high school classmates voted me "most likely to succeed." They also chose me to be homecoming queen – an extraordinary achievement for a woman of color in a predominantly white Denver high school. Though I have worn a crown, a "unicorn" crown, many times in my life, I didn't feel like that "queen" on the inside. I came from modest means, but I had a compelling drive. My family didn't summer on Martha's Vineyard; they weren't members of the famed Talented tenth; they didn't leave me wealth or a singular pedigree or a roadmap toward business leadership. I had an unfettered drive to create my own. But I do credit those friends and colleagues — many of them my role models — who gave me nudges along the way. Some were hard; some were gentle.

Jackie's Story—Education and Excellence

My first role models were my maternal grandparents. Their achievements in the earliest years of the 20th century, despite widespread and dehumanizing Jim Crow restrictions, were and remain remarkable. I have always felt blessed to have their DNA and a responsibility to live up to their examples.

Triby Jane Thompson Colbert, my grandmother, was a teacher and the daughter of a slave, who was born around 1844. According to a family history compiled in 2004, Louis Thompson was deliberately secretive about his background. He migrated from Virginia to northeastern Louisiana, where he purchased land in 1887 and 1897 and became a successful farmer and businessman.

Dr. Benjamin Luther Colbert, my grandfather, earned his doctorate in veterinary medicine from Ohio State University. Family legend has it that he earned an additional Ph.D. working with Tuskegee Institute's famed Dr. George Washington Carver. When I knew him, my grandfather taught agriculture to high school students in Atlanta and tended a large, luxurious garden in his backyard. I still have my grandmother's Waterford crystal punch bowl, which, to me, symbolizes her sense of style and reflects her physical beauty.

My mother attended Spelman College but left school a few weeks before graduation because of a spat over a cotillion dress. Apparently, she felt that as a senior, she should have gotten a new gown instead of her younger sister who was just a junior. As a child, I played dress–up in the several formal gowns that my mother had acquired, never realizing how few mothers, of any color, had attended cotillions. She followed classmates to Boston where she met and married my father, Grady Lassiter Adams, who was a licensed practical nurse.

Like Bonita's family, we lived a comfortable, middle–class life. My parents owned their own home, and I recall being cranky because my mother didn't wear pearls like June Cleaver when she vacuumed. Unlike Bonita, I was not rewarded with cash for good grades. But I earned them anyway, in the belief that love was equated with achievement.

My earliest memory is of my father saying, "When you're Black in America, to be equal, you have to be superior." He wasn't the first or the last African American parent to outline this particular path to power or even just survival. Instead of balking at the inherent unfairness of that recipe for success, i.e., my father's acknowledgment of institutional racism, I said to myself, "Is that all it takes?" After all, the world's standard of success – of passing a course – is just a C. How much more energy does it take to work a little harder to get an A? And so I did.

I earned a perfect score of 800 on my Latin college admission test. I graduated second in my class from the prestigious Girls' Latin School in Boston. My guidance counselor had bellowed in her Boston Brahmin accent, "You, my dear, must attend a Seven Sister college, one of the elite women's colleges." And so I did. I was admitted early decision to the only college to which I applied, Barnard College.

My high school yearbook asked each student for an ambition. I loved history and writing and admired Barbara Walters when she interviewed politicians and authors every morning on NBC News. That's why I wrote that my ambition was to be the "girl on The

Today Show." *Clearly, I wasn't very "woke" in 1968, but I came pretty close to achieving that childhood goal. There were no newscasters of color at that time, but I didn't see my race or gender as a barrier. Perhaps I had a failure of imagination, or perhaps I was shielded from the so–called real world in a cocoon of education and expectations of excellence.*

My father had strong views on a range of topics, and they forced me to become an independent thinker, and to trust my inner voice more than that of anyone else. He didn't believe in clothing fads. His mantra was: "If you wear good conservative clothes, you'll always be in style." It turns out he was right, but I recall my deep dismay when I wasn't able to buy a Dr. Kildare shirt as a teenager, even though every one of my classmates had one.

My father never let me or my younger brother go trick or treating on Halloween. We had costumes for the parties in nursery school, and we could get dressed up to answer the door to hand out candy on October 31. But my father was both firm and proud. He saw "trick or treating" as a form of begging. "If my children need candy," he would say, "I will buy it for them myself."

My father was quite proud of something else, which may seem minor in hindsight. I never went to school with a peanut butter and jelly sandwich. My father insisted I always have a meat sandwich. It might have been Balogna rather than roast beef or ham. He never used the word protein, *but he saw my lunches as markers of his ability to provide for his family.*

He also told me, within my mother's hearing, that he never wanted me to grow up to become "just some man's wife." He proved it by frequently liberating me from ironing or vacuuming when I wanted to read rather than do housework. If my mother objected, she didn't say much. All I recall her saying was that it was easy to get married. "Anyone can do it."

If you examine the broad strokes, I have always gotten all as, worn good conservative clothes and heeded my inner voice. I have lived what I would call a golden life. I have worked extraordinarily hard. Optimism and zest have been my hallmarks, along with grit. My glass has always been more than half–full. Being happy and grateful for my blessings, I feel, has generated them.

Twin Tragedies

Both of us were "daddy's girls," which made our fathers' untimely deaths even more searing. We share the unfortunate coincidence of losing our fathers to heart disease when we both were in college. Coincidentally, both men were just 47 years old when they passed, compounding our twin tragedies.

Bonita was a freshman. Jackie was a senior. Neither of our fathers was able to see or share directly in our professional successes. Our losses made us dig deep within our souls. We each had lost emotional and financial safety nets. Each of us quickly realized no one else was going to take care of us as our fathers had. Our mothers were archetypal nice ladies, but our fathers had been the sparks, the inspiration and intellectual drivers of our young lives.

In our *Women of Color in Business: Cross Generational Survey©*, we asked our respondents about the role their parents played in their early development. It was no surprise that a huge majority of our 4,005 women cited their mothers as major influences. What was interesting, though, was that African American women and LatinX women whose fathers were strong role models were more likely to earn more money. Women of all races who cited the strong influence of fathers were 15% more likely to have earned a college degree or more.

FATHER AS A ROLE MODEL

Linked to wealth
Black and LatinX women whose fathers were role models while they grew up are more likely to have higher incomes.

Leads to higher education
Women of all races who cite their fathers as role models are 15% more likely to have a college degree or higher, and 56% earn college degrees.

Women of Color in Business: Cross Generational Survey©

Despite our tragedies, we remained optimistic about our futures, confident we both could achieve the goals about which we had dreamed. Despite our tragedies, we knew we were blessed with grit, perseverance, optimism, intelligence and now perhaps an even more fierce determination to succeed–to succeed for two–for ourselves and our fathers.

In the mid–1980s, Bonita found her life compass, concrete "blessings," when she returned to South Carolina to sort out her family's real estate holdings. Going through her grandmother's belongings, she found two earth–shattering but spirit–lifting documents among a rather messy pile of papers.

The first was a letter her father wrote to his mother on the day she was born. The letter mostly gushed about their new baby girl whom he described as "just out of this world." Signed as "loving son–J," Bonita was struck by her father's gentleness and pride as he described how he and her older brother (two at the time) were "running the house" as he was on leave. The pedestal on which Bonita had placed her father grew taller as she held concrete evidence of his experiences as an ideal son, husband and father.

The second document was even more profound and life–changing. It was a remarkable, wide–ranging essay that Bonita's father had written, called "The Trail to Success." John Coleman, Jr. had been certified as a teacher in South Carolina after receiving his Bachelor of Arts from Benedict College in 1950, but like many men his age, he enrolled in the armed services and married his hometown sweetheart in 1954. His entry was post–military integration which was issued as an executive order by President Truman in July 1948.[27] Credit has been given to the Secretary of the Air Force, W. Stuart Symington, who moved quickly to break up the Black units. The Air Force became the first military branch to complete integration.

Sometimes, you have to believe you are lucky or timing works in your favor. It was a tough transition as John Coleman, Jr., forged his "only" path, becoming an officer and persisting in his own way to train as a pilot. Family lore said he applied for pilot training school numerous times, until the day his superiors didn't crumple up his application. By 1960, he had completed pilot training for the B–47, the first supersonic nuclear bomber, including technical and related nuclear weapons schools. He went on to complete his engineering school training for the B–58 Hustler, the first operational bomber capable of Mach 2 flight.

The rest, as they say, was history. His essay revealed an extraordinarily sweeping embrace of history, religion and poetry. His patriotism was unremarkable, given his profession. But clearly, he loved the United States even more than the country, and its politicians loved people who looked like him.

The essay breathed life into Bonita's calling—being an owner, a leader and a boss. In it, her father outlined his Four Cs: Character, Concentration, Culture and Courage.

Bonita—The Impact of The Trail to Success

Throughout my life, I have unpacked the Four Cs and used them at various times to make critical decisions. Here's just one example:

When I was recruited to join Chrysler as the head of Consumer Strategy, I knew from my experience that technology would become an enabler of a new, more disruptive consumer buying experience. It was my "concentration" in the business of technology that focused me on new ideas such as pursuing a CarMax partnership and experimenting with new consumer–centric technology. When I left in 2000 to follow my natural calling to join the era of the Wild Wild Web, I felt it was important to "leave well." Mindful of my father's focus on "character," I wrote personal notes to every senior executive who had provided a guiding hand or intellectual learning opportunity to aid my business growth. Less than two years later, we went full circle, and I was recruited by the senior executives and CEO Dieter Zetsche to return as the head of Chrysler Brand Advertising.

With my deepest pride, I share with you "The Trail to Success" as penned by John W. Coleman, Jr. I hope that you can experience even an ounce of my jubilation in finding this treasure map. I hope that it brings you the same blessings and the same inspiration that it has brought me!

The Trail to Success

To every conscientious person who stands on the threshold of life's career, there comes the all-important question: "How shall I attain success?" We can look back to our young days when our lives were full of play and hours of ease. Though pleasing memories, they are, we realize, forever past.

You as young people should focus your thoughts on the days you are now spending in school, though lessons may be hard and discipline severe. You must now realize that they are precious and important moments. All of you will not have the chance to attend college after completion of your high school work, and then you must make your debut into this drama of life on the basis of your achievements in high school. But those of you who will be given the opportunity to further your knowledge before making your debut into this drama of life should be grateful.

To each of these individuals who is about to make his debut into this drama of life, to each of these conscientious persons who is about to throw himself into the world of affairs, there comes the omnipotent questions: "How can I attain success?" "What can I do as my bit in helping to advance my fellow man?" "What path shall I pursue to be on the true trail of success?"

Permit me at this moment to make myself clear just what I mean by success. Webster defines success as "a favorable termination of anything attempted." Accepting that definition at its face value, anyone who has decided to make his living by gambling or bootlegging, and succeeding in doing so, can claim success for himself. But I don't mean that kind of success. When I use the word success, I mean accomplishing something for the benefit of Christian civilization and fallen humanity. In other words, I do not mean to regard one's life as a success, even though he does accomplish that which he desires, unless those desires are in accord with the life and teachings of our Lord and Savior Jesus Christ.

Coming again to the question: "How can one make life a success? To do anything, there are certain rules and regulations that we must be governed by. To be a banker, one must abide by the laws of finance and commerce. To have a strong and healthy body, one must abide by the "laws of nutrition."

To make one's life a success, one must abide by the rules of and follow in the paths of those whose lives have been successes. In my estimation, four fundamental necessities are prerequisites to any successful career. Also, there are four elements that pave the way on what I have chosen to designate as "The Trail to Success."

The first element I would name is Concentration. If one would succeed in life, he must concentrate all his talents and energy on one specific object. The Apostle Paul said, "This one thing I do." Joshua said, "Choose you this day what God you will serve." If one wishes to succeed, he must do one thing at a time, for better to do one thing and do it well than attempt a dozen and leave them all half-finished. Having concentrated upon one object, one must develop his talents.

Culture is the second element essential for one to be on the true trail to success. May I remind you that fine fruit does not grow on uncultured trees. The digging may be deep, the pruning may be severe, but the quality of the fruit obtained will justify the labor and the pain.

The third element is Courage! When I say courage, I don't mean that something that makes us act on the spur of the moment, either by passion, emotion or fear. I mean courage like that Abraham Lincoln possessed — courage, which helped him to face life with a determination — that courage thatcarried him from rail-splitter

38

to the presidency of our country. When I say courage, I mean that courage that makes it pleasant for the burdened masses of people to sing a song of joy, to hope for better days as they bear the drudgery of their daily toil. Courage like that of the pioneers of these United States: To defy the barren wastes and perilous journeys of an uncivilized land, to defy the unjust laws of a mother country and establish this our America — This our United States — Youngest, but Greatest.

I mean courage like that of our forefathers held just a few years ago — courage to hope and pray while bound fast in the chains of slavery and afar being emancipated, without clothes, wealth, education, without food and the majority without a place to lay their heads — Courage to pray — to work and rise to the height of the present American Negro — fifteen million strong — a record unsurpassed.

Courage to face life, determined to succeed, regardless of our color. God likes colors. That's why he gave us the many hues in flowers as well as in individuals. And if the world were truly Christian, there would be no serious problem as to the color of the skin one possesses. A person would be assayed solely based on what constructive work he could perform during his lifetime. Psychologists have taught that the true measure of a man consists of his products rather than his complexion. "What can you do"? is the real test of your worth, instead of "what is your race and color?"

In short, can you "do" something that is commendable? You can't even be good unless you "do" good, for virtue is measured only by actions and deeds.

Last but not least, I would like to put into this structure, character. When I use the word Character, I mean that kind of character that will coincide with the life and teaching of Christ. Success can never be obtained without the foundation of a true and noble character. One man said, "Character is power." J. Hawes said, "The character is like white paper. If once blotted, it can hardly ever be made to appear white as before. One wrong step often stains the character for life. It is much easier to form a good character and preserve it pure, than to purify it after it has become defiled." Therefore, if one wishes to attain the envious bliss of success, he must travel the path — The Trail to Success — armed with concentration, culture, courage and character. And if armed with these essential elements — at the end of the trail will stand that long-sought goal — success.

Not the evil success of which I spoke of in the beginning but the true Christian success, the likes of which I shall attempt to describe:

It's doing your work the best you can
And being just to your fellow man
It's making money and holding friends
And staying true to your aims and ends;
It's figuring how and learning why,
And looking forward and thinking high,
And dreaming a little and doing much
It's keeping always in closest touch;
With what is finest in word and deed;
It's being thorough yet making speed,
It's daring blithely the field of chance
While making labor a bright romance,
It's going onward despite defeat
And fighting staunchly, but keeping sweet
It's being clean and it's playing fair
It's laughing lightly at despair
It's looking up at the stars above
It's drinking deeply of life and love
It's struggling onward with the will to win

40

But taking loss with a cheerful grin
It's showing sorrow and work and worth
And making better this good old earth
It's serving, striving, through strain and stress
In doing your noblest – "That's Success."
J.W. Coleman, Jr. 1928-1975

Copyright© 1999

Our Legacy

On paper and by example, our families left both of us with legacies of resilience and the tools to pursue excellence through education and hard work.

Yes, at the beginning of our careers, we were often "onlys," decades before researchers uncovered the psychological costs of being such. We didn't count or hold grudges over what are now called "microaggressions." When or if we faced race–based obstacles, they were MACRO–aggressions.

If we are brutally honest, we may have actually enjoyed our solitary status at times. We may have bought into the perception of "risk" that has often been associated with a crowd of people of color in any work setting, but especially in a corporate setting. Could it be a vestigial instinct or ancient memory from slavery times – the danger of a group plotting escape or revolution?

Who knows? Now, even if it is belatedly, we have embraced "the blessing," which is the definition of a crowd of unicorns, a gathering of huge numbers of achieving women of color. And today, we are determined to use our natural grit to explain and share how we did what we've done.

Our mission is larger, however. In addition to sharing our own stories, we are amplifying this conversation digitally to

41

empower other women of color to team up, to work together, to include others, to pay it forward so any woman can achieve success—on her own terms.

Ironically, what initially drove and sustained both of us has been the wisdom of our fathers. John W. Coleman, Jr. and Grady Adams gave us what we needed, and we are giving it to you.

Throughout our chapters, we have noted examples of grit, optimism resilience and especially gratitude in our personal stories. And we have begun to develop what we call a **Living Log**, both here and on our website: www.LeadEmpowerThrive.com.

The **Log** contains thought—provoking questions, suggestions and even resources. This Log is for YOU. We see this as not only a Living Log but an Actionable Log.

 **LIVING LOG**

❑ How do you define "grit?"
❑ Take five minutes to think of a time when you brought your "grit" to life. How did you activate your superpower? Through yourself? Or from others?
❑ Do you know how to use "grit" when it is most needed?
❑ Do you know the difference between confidence and arrogance?
❑ How often do you feel—and express—gratitude?

❑ How can you trigger "optimism" in times of doubt or disappointment?
❑ Do you express gratitude or thanks whenever someone helps you or even just offers to help?
❑ Who are your role models? Think of people in your own family or figures from history or popular culture.
❑ Build your network of "gritty" folks and read inspirational stories about thriving.
❑ Some of our recent favorites include:
  ❑ *Becoming* by Michelle Obama
  ❑ *The Memo* by Minda Hart
  ❑ *More than Enough* by Elaine Welteroth
  ❑ *Just Mercy: A Story of Justice and Redemption* by Bryan Stephenson
  ❑ *The Year of Yes: How to Dance It Out, Stand in the Sun and Be Your Own Person by Shonda Rhimes*
  ❑ *Race, Work, and Leadership: New Perspectives on the Black Experience* by Laura Morgan Roberts, Anthony Mayo and David Thomas
  ❑ *How Children Succeed: Grit, Curiosity and the Hidden Power of Character* by Paul Tough
  ❑ *Climb: Taking Every Step With Conviction, Courage and Calculated RIsks to Achieve a Throiving Career and a Successful Life* by Michelle Gadsden–Williams
  ❑ *Primitive: Tapping the Primal Drive that Powers the World's Most Successful People* by Marco Greenberg

What books or articles or podcasts would you add to this list?

Chapter Two

The Power of Value

The dictionary defines "power" in two distinctly different ways. It is "the capacity or ability to direct or influence the behavior of others or the course of events." But power is also "physical strength and force exerted by something or someone."

In this book, particularly in this chapter, the word "power" similarly has two different meanings. Enslaved people possessed great physical power, but it was not used to influence or enrich themselves. Instead, the power of enslaved people was directed against them individually, in support of the goals and enrichment of their owners.

Our challenge today is to decouple the meanings, to recognize the physical, emotional and historical strengths of women of color, to use our "power" collectively and individually for good.

Similarly, influence has two meanings. As a noun, it means "the capacity to have an effect on the character, development or behavior of someone or something, or the effect itself." As a verb, however, influence means "determine, guide, direct, affect, shape, govern, regulate, change." It is a very active verb.

Again, our enslaved ancestors were kept from exerting their influence directly. But their blood runs in our veins and today, women of color are exerting influence, "shaping" and "changing" themselves and the world in ways as myriad as the shades of their skin.

Power, Gender and Race

In the leadup to 2020's centennial celebrations of the passage of the 19th Amendment to the U.S. Constitution giving women the right to vote, some analysts have argued that the word "power" is gendered. Think of men and power. Images come to mind of generals and political leaders, captains of industry, religious leaders and their accompanying strength, success, ambition and even financial might. Think of women and power. Traditionally, the images have been much less positive: rhymes with witch, pushy, brash, unladylike, unlikeable and the dreaded "angry."

Experts cite the famous New York University study in which undergraduates were asked to review nearly identical profiles for employees holding the position of assistant vice president for sales in an aircraft company. The major difference between the employees is that one was named "James" and the other was named "Andrea." Both were in the top five percent in employee performance reviews and both were described as "stellar performers" or "rising stars." The profiles provided no background on their personality or character. And yet, the students rated "Andrea" as more disagreeable and uncivil than "James," who got more glowing responses.[28] Imagine the reactions if the names had been "Jamal" or "Aisha." Over the last two decades, several studies at Harvard and UCLA have quantified negative, biased reactions to Black–sounding names.[29]

It would seem as if the deck is stacked against a woman of color, especially one with an ethnic–sounding name. How is she to avoid being penalized for being as ambitious, direct and strategic as a "James?" How is she to claim her power, to use her power successfully? Here's one example:

Depelsha McGruder—Cultural Bias

Attending an executive education program at a well–known management school, HBS alum Depelsha McGruder reported on her Facebook page that she participated in a session called "Assessing Your Networks."

In preparation, we had to complete an online assessment in advance about our personal and professional networks that took about 20 to 30 minutes. One of the final questions on the assessment was, "How many people do you know well named Emily, Alan or Rachel?" We were asked to count the number of people with these particular names that we could contact quickly (without searching or going to social media). I found this an odd question but just answered it and moved on. Once in class, we learned that THIS question was used to estimate the breadth and size of our networks. The computer literally generated a number based on how many Emilys, Alans and Rachels we know.

This prompted me to raise my hand. 👩🏿‍🦱 👤 ☐ to say, "This question is culturally biased. As a person of color, I have a large, powerful network that does not include many people named Emily, Alan or Rachel. The Mayor of Atlanta is named KEISHA. I happen to know quite a few powerful Keishas who are not reflected in this network assessment. So I don't think this methodology is valid for people of color." International students piled on, pointing out the various ways the assessment is also invalid globally (including how people define acquaintance vs. colleague vs. friend, etc. differently). It was a teachable moment for the class and the professor (who put up a feeble attempt to convince me that Emily, Alan and Rachel are statistically proven to be the most race–neutral names and the most common names in the U.S.). The class had my back, and they've been thanking me all evening at dinner for speaking up!

Atta–girl, Depelsha! Increasingly, women of color are speaking up, owning their power and asserting their influence.

Women of Color in Business—Cross Generational Survey© Results

Indeed, our proprietary survey of 4,005 cross–generational women of color "desk" or knowledge workers found that all of the women—Black, white, Asian and Latinx—offered advice that would support the actions Depelsha took in her executive education classroom: Work hard, never give up, be yourself!

When we asked about workplace confidence and career flexibility, there were only two groups of outliers. Older, Boomer Asian (53%) and white (55%) desk workers said they were pessimistic about their chances of finding another good job easily.

However, Black and LatinX workers of all generations as well as younger, Generation Z, Millennial and Generation X Asian and white women are all confident that they do and will have control of their careers. They say they could find other good jobs easily, ignoring the naysayers and past history.

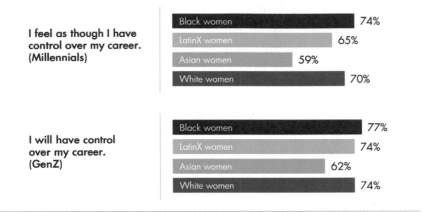

I feel as though I have control over my career. (Millennials)
- Black women 74%
- LatinX women 65%
- Asian women 59%
- White women 70%

I will have control over my career. (GenZ)
- Black women 77%
- LatinX women 74%
- Asian women 62%
- White women 74%

Women of Color in Business: Cross Generational Survey©

I could find another good job relatively easily.

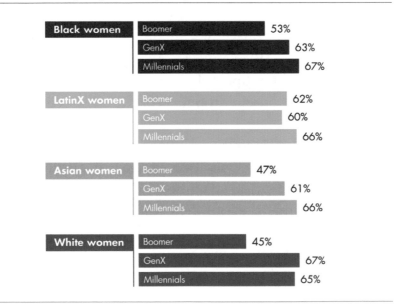

Black women
- Boomer 53%
- GenX 63%
- Millennials 67%

LatinX women
- Boomer 62%
- GenX 60%
- Millennials 66%

Asian women
- Boomer 47%
- GenX 61%
- Millennials 66%

White women
- Boomer 45%
- GenX 67%
- Millennials 65%

Women of Color in Business: Cross Generational Survey©

This evidence confirms the optionality that our younger women of all colors feel. They reject any vestige of 21st century enslavement. Their confidence should give employers and prospective employers pause. These women feel they can reject any form of intolerance they might find in the workplace. They can and will leave an employer whose values do not dovetail with theirs.

The Meaning of Value

African Americans have always been valuable. When we were first brought to North America in 1619, we were physical capital. More recently, we have begun to exercise the power, influence and economic freedom, that accompany that value.

According to the 1860 census, enslaved people were valued at $3.1 billion, roughly the equivalent of the value of all the capital invested in manufacturing, railroads, banks and currency then in circulation.[30]

Researchers calculate that in the first 60 years of the 19th century, before the Civil War, raw cotton represented more than half of all U.S. exports and of course, cotton was grown almost exclusively by enslaved people.[31] The value of slaves continues to provide teachable moments, although perhaps not the ones we might want to teach.

Depelsha McGruder revealed in another of her Facebook posts that middle school teachers in Missouri and North Carolina have been teaching fractions by asking students to calculate how many slaves it would take to equal four white people.[32] She also shared a Minnesota Public Radio

49

podcast and news report that uncovered how our modern accounting system (i.e. debit, credit, depreciation) was based on the accounting methods used during slavery to keep track of the sales and valuation of slaves.[33]

Branding and the Enslaved

Yes, enslaved people had tremendous value and, by extension, tremendous power. Given the stakes, it's no wonder the media, for centuries, has worked overtime to brand people of color as subhuman. If we were perceived as fully human with souls and aspirations, it was harder to exploit us. If we ourselves perceived our full value and power, we might be dangerous.

Abolitionist Frederick Douglass made it his business to correct the image. Throughout the second half of the 19th century, Douglass was the most photographed man in America. Harvard Professor Henry Louis Gates, Jr., has written that Douglass' specific goal was to use the new technology of photography to counter the "racist stereotypes, 'the already read text' of the debased, subhuman Negro fabricated and so profusely distributed by the slave power, by supplanting those images with a proliferation of anti–caricatures."[34]

At the same time, many Black women activists were also photographed. Among them were educators Hallie Quinn Brown and Clarissa M. Thompson. The Library of Congress has recently digitized images of these women, making them widely available to see and admire.

Look at their stylish hats and hairstyles and jewelry. Who could consider any of these beautiful and powerful women "debased" or "subhuman?" To see the intelligence in their eyes, to study these survivors of slavery and Jim Crow runs counter to the white nationalist attempt to brand people/women of color as less than. Who wouldn't feel proud that these women were our sisters, our role models, truly our mothers, who survived and triumphed under conditions far more painful and constricting than anything we experience today.[35]

Fast forward to 2018, when Nielsen reported African Americans were responsible for some $1.2 trillion in annual purchases, even though we are just 14% of the population. Black consumers make up over 50% of overall spending on dry grains and vegetables as well as baby food (42.76%) personal soap and bath needs (41.64%) and air fresheners and deodorizers (38.29%). Researchers also say Black consumer choices have a "cool factor" that creates a halo effect and strongly impacts the mainstream.[36]

Our *Women of Color in Business: Cross Generational Survey©* survey confirmed the Nielsen findings. Among all the women who are "always the first to know when something new or cutting edge in technology is released," 31% of the Black and LatinX women overall said yes, 26% for Asian women and just 19% for white women.

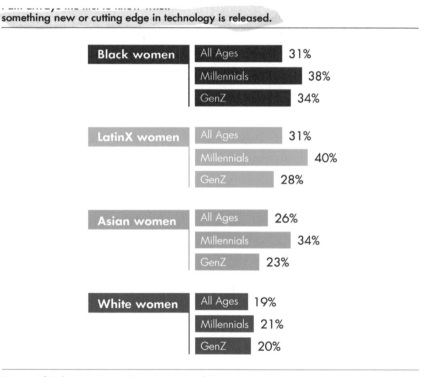

something new or cutting edge in technology is released.

Black women	All Ages	31%
	Millennials	38%
	GenZ	34%
LatinX women	All Ages	31%
	Millennials	40%
	GenZ	28%
Asian women	All Ages	26%
	Millennials	34%
	GenZ	23%
White women	All Ages	19%
	Millennials	21%
	GenZ	20%

Women of Color in Business: Cross Generational Survey©

The numbers were particularly striking for Gen Z and Millennial women–34% and 38% for Blacks and 29% and 40% for LatinX. More Asian Millennial women agreed at 34%. Again, white women lagged at 19% and 21%, respectively.

Beyond the raw numbers, digital technology has added to the power of female consumers of color. No longer need we be "over–served" by nervous shopkeepers. Shopping online means "shopping incognito." For many brands, we have become coveted trendsetters.

40 Acres—40 Allies

Imagine how much more valuable, more valued and more powerful people of color would be if our great–grandparents had received the "40 acres and a mule" they were promised at the end of the Civil War. Instead, we've had to "make a way out of no way." We're still here; we're optimistic about our futures; and many of us are crushing it. But there could be a new paradigm: "40 allies and a stretch assignment." This is Bonita's business fantasy.

We would provide each woman of color with land–or allies–who would nurture her growth and a mule–or a stretch assignment–to test the strength of her capabilities.

What is a stretch assignment? I define it as a new position, a new opportunity that must scare you a little. If it doesn't scare you, it's not really a stretch. It could be a global assignment or an assignment in a male–dominated area of a business or an emerging business area. It's an assignment that will differentiate your résumé and if–no, WHEN you succeed–your allies and perhaps even your detractors will have no option other than to call you a "force of nature."

I see this formula–40 allies and stretch assignment–being used selectively across our known "Black unicorns." But imagine the progress we'd make if we could scale this model. As Robert F.

Smith, CEO of Vista Equity Partners and a fellow Denverite stated in The Economist (The World in 2020): *"In 2020, it is time to reassess the American Dream. Redesigning the American Dream requires each of us to pry open these windows of opportunity in big ways and small."*

With a defining opportunity embraced by a posse of allies across all industries, women of color would take major steps toward building power, power defined as value creation for themselves and others. With value creation comes influence, and with influence comes freedom.

In hindsight, Bonita has experienced the "40 allies and a stretch assignment" fantasy she now envisions for other women of color in business.

As I look back, my personal value creation came from my multiple allies and in every case, a defining assignment. Whether it was being hired by IBM during a hiring freeze, starting my own business (twice), working with the scrappy IBM PC team, leading Chrysler Brand advertising, running Chrysler/Dodge/Jeep digital marketing or launching Google's automotive practice, these were all game–changing adventures. What goes hand in hand with value creation is collaboration and, ultimately, economic freedom. As African Americans, we have had our most defining and finest hours when we collaborated and supported one another as we designed the Underground Railroad, marched on Selma and rallied to support America's first African American president.

When we asked HBS alum Zuhairah Scott Washington about stretch assignments, this Senior Vice President, Global Head of Strategic Accounts/Partnerships at a Fortune 500 travel technology company, laughed.

All I seem to take on are stretch assignments, and they are nearly impossible without adequate management support. As a person of color, you need to differentiate yourself, and I've found that stretch assignments can offer unique opportunities to catapult your career. When you find a way to achieve what others deem impossible, unexpected or unlikely, people have a reason to believe in you and begin to rely more on you to drive results in the future. But it can't happen too early in your career. You need both the inner confidence as well as credibility within your organization to pull one of these off.

The best bosses, the best allies (and most of mine have been men, both Black and white) do three things:

- *A boss who supports you is taking a risk on you, giving you the opportunity to grow;*
- *S/he provides reinforcing feedback; and*
- *S/he's advocating for you in the rooms where big decisions are made.*

I have found that bosses who don't do these three things are often the ones who are less secure within themselves. They buckle under the pressure of being at the top, and as a result, they are the ones who haven't operated at their best for me or for themselves.

Don't Let Ambition Be Derailed

Similar to the familiar business and political phrase, "don't let a good crisis go to waste," let's not let the ambition of women of color be derailed. In our *Women of Color in Business: Cross Generational Survey©*, we found 58% of Black women vs. 54% of white women feel as though they have made a strong contribution in the jobs they've had. The numbers are not that different.

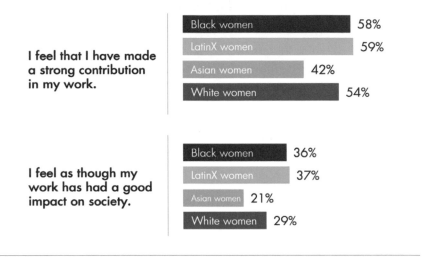

I feel that I have made a strong contribution in my work.

Black women	58%
LatinX women	59%
Asian women	42%
White women	54%

I feel as though my work has had a good impact on society.

Black women	36%
LatinX women	37%
Asian women	21%
White women	29%

Women of Color in Business: Cross Generational Survey©

A major difference emerged, however, when we asked if the women thought their work had a good impact on society more broadly. 36% of Black women vs. 29% of white women had that view.

Jackie—Social Good

During my career at CBS News, I was told the network's founder, William S. Paley, intended for the news division to be a loss leader. He didn't expect it to make money. Other program-ming—comedies, like I Love Lucy, *or dramas, like* Gunsmoke– *could make the money. But the news was to be a sacred space, a public trust, if not a public service.*

In the 1980s, that philosophy disappeared, and a more typical business perspective was adopted. News became a profit center.

*And that change impacted both the types of stories that were select-
ed and the way those stories were covered. Reporters and producers
had to justify spending money on travel to news events. Big stories
came to dominate coverage, in part to spread the costs over the
budgets of the special events "breaking news" department as well
as daily news coverage. The OJ Simpson murder trials were among
the first examples of this change. Today, we can cite examples like
the 2020 pandemic coverage and the presidential campaigns.*

*For me, though, the old–fashioned attitude of "service" or
educating the public animated my original interest in being a jour-
nalist. When the philosophy changed, I looked for ways to continue
linking my work with my interest in providing a social good.*

*When I left CBS News and became an entrepreneur, I deliber-
ately chose to "work for pay" only half–time. I chose to "pay to
work" with the rest of my time, i.e., volunteering in a variety of
non–profit organizations that tracked with the types of stories I had
covered: foreign policy, the arts and education. The reason I could
pursue this strategy was because I redefined what "enough" meant
in terms of my income. Because I had a bit of a nest egg and hadn't
had children who might have needed expensive educations, I had
the economic freedom to follow my passions.*

Such freedom, though, is in short supply for most people of color.

Quantifying the Racial Wealth Gap

For better or worse, communities of color remain the
places where there is almost no money — still. The statistics for African American entrepreneurs seeking angel and
venture financing are beyond shocking.

A 2018 study from ProjectDiane, created in collaboration
with JPMorgan Chase, the Case Foundation and the Ewing

Marion Kauffman Foundation, found that the number of startups founded by Black women has more than doubled in two years. There were 227 startups in the ProjectDiane 2018 database compared to 84 in 2016, a 2.5 times increase. However, the median funding raised by all Black women founders was $0. That's zero dollars.

While there was a growing number of Black women crossing the million–dollar venture threshold, the vast majority of Black women–led startups has been unable to raise any money. Black women have raised only .0006% of the $424.7 billion in total, tech venture funding raised since 2009.[37]

McKinsey & Co. released a major study in August 2019 about the causes of the persistent U.S. racial wealth gap. The conclusion is, if the gap were closed, the United States' gross domestic product would rise by up to 6% by 2028 through increased investments and consumption. That 6% translates into an additional $1+ trillion.

Among the most striking findings are those about Black women and Black families.[38]

- The median wealth of a single Black woman is $200, compared with the median wealth of a single white man, which is $28,900. The reasons for the disparity include higher levels of debt, especially student loan debt, and lower incomes.
- Black women earn 89% as much as Black men, who earn only 74% at the median as white men. This dual wage penalty means the median Black woman earns only 65% as much as the median white man.

- A typical Black family has only one–sixth of the liquid savings of a white family. Even a Black family's support network is poorer. In an emergency, most Black families would not know someone who could lend them $3,000.
- As of 2016, the wealth of the average white family was 10 times higher than the average wealth of a Black family. The white household had a net worth of $171,000 while average Black and Hispanic households had a median net worth of $17,600 and $20,700, respectively.
- Only 8% of Black families receive an inheritance, compared with 26% of white families. When an inheritance does come, it is 35% of the value of that of a white family.
- Only 40% of Black families own a home, compared with 73% of white families.
- As of 2016, 67% of Black Americans had incomes of at least $50,000 invested in the stock market or mutual funds, compared with 86% of white Americans.
- Only 7% of Black Americans' assets are in business equity (often a product of entrepreneurship), compared with 16% for white families.

Although our *Women of Color in Business: Cross Generational Survey*© found tremendous optimism about the future overall among our 4,005 respondents, there was one major area of pessimism and dissatisfaction. Only 21% of the women overall said they were satisfied with their ability "to earn and save as much as they would like for the lifestyle they want."

The statistics were most dismal for older, Boomer women (ages 55–72): Black 13%, LatinX 22%, Asian 23% and white 13%.

I am satisfied with my ability to earn and save for the lifestyle I want.

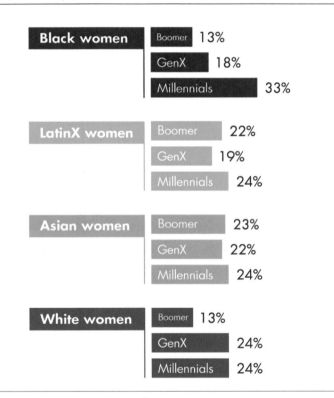

Women of Color in Business: Cross Generational Survey©

Generation X (ages 38–54) was slightly better: Black 18%, LatinX 19%, Asian 22% and white 24%.

And Millennials (ages 23–37) are even more satisfied, especially Black Millennials 33%, LatinX 24%, Asian 24% and white 24%.

Let's Sit on Our Sofa— Advice for Earning and Saving

Offering advice, particularly about money, is a tricky, potentially dangerous topic. However, neither of us is as unhappy as the women in our age group in our survey, so we're going to take a stab at it.

Start saving something, any amount, as early as you can. A place to start, to calculate how much to save, is the wealth calculator tool on the Calculate My Wealth website: http://calculatemywealth.com/wealth–calculator/.

Type in your age, the age at which you want to retire, how much you have already saved for retirement and the amount you can invest each month. The calculator will tell you what you'll acquire if you rely on a savings account, if you invest half your money in the stock market, or if you invest all of your savings in the stock market. In the interest of full transparency, this tool and website are the work of Bonita's husband, Kevin Stewart.

Kevin felt if we had the basics early in life and understood the power of equity markets, we would build wealth from day one. For example:

- You are 25.
- You want to retire at 62.
- You have already saved $2,000.
- Going forward, you plan to invest $500 a month.
- If you put all of your cash into stocks with an average 10%* growth = $2,373,749 of savings. (*Source: Standard and Poor's, January 1970 through the end of 2012)

- If you just put your cash in a bank savings (2% interest based on prior historical levels) = $332,897 of savings.
- If you put half your cash into a savings account and half in stocks (around 6% growth) = $831,835 of savings.

The key variable for how much you're willing to invest in stocks, or which kinds of stocks and index funds, is your tolerance for risk. Tolerance is variable, strictly personal and can vary depending on where we are in the overall business cycle. Some people think investing in the midst of a recession is a good place to find bargains. But risk, some risk, is a prerequisite for an "abundance mindset."

While we're on our soapbox, we suggest you set up an "emergency only" fund for house or car repairs, health emergencies or family emergencies. We also suggest that you practice gratitude for what you already have.

Both of us have grown up in traditional, middleclass families. We learned the value of homeownership and savings from our parents, grandparents and great–grandparents. Sadly, little has been written or studied about the experiences of families like ours. So, we are presenting our histories and perspectives on money. We have also added the hard–nosed advice about various asset classes from a dear friend, a self–made millionaire, Paula.

Bonita–Appreciable Assets

Power, Influence, and Freedom (PIF) seem to go together like a well–worn charm bracelet. I see them as the lucky charms for career ascension, confidence and redemption.

At an early age, I learned the importance of having financial freedom. As children, my brothers and I were each given a nominal allowance for the performance of chores as a means to teach us a strong work ethic. My father would repeatedly say, "Money doesn't grow on trees." Being the curious one, I researched and found real money vs. subsidized household labor grew from having a real job. As a reputable babysitter, I did quite well around the neighborhood. However, when the job expectation expanded beyond just babysitting to house cleaning too, I was out. It was time for a career switch!

While I hate to admit this, since I don't like fast food at all, I took a job at McDonald's at age 16. I did this to have more financial independence. McDonald's was the only family–friendly company hiring high school teens with zero experience. After receiving a real paycheck, I learned the power of cumulative savings. I remember the store manager distinctly, and I always thought I could do a better job running the joint. After learning many of the roles in the kitchen and offering operational suggestions to increase our store revenue, my manager immediately moved me to the front as a cashier, and I was ringing it in. Without knowing it then, I learned the power of the upsell.

From that day on, I realized the power financial freedom brings. While I enjoyed treating myself to the movies, the latest fashion apparel and helping others, I found the most satisfaction witnessing firsthand the power of compound interest and delayed gratification. I was dreaming bigger than my parents could ever imagine, yet I am forever grateful for their sacrifices. In their minds, they escaped the South, owned their four–bedroom home with stunning Rocky Mountain views in a highly respectable, predominantly white neighborhood, with the best public school in Denver county.

They owned everything–their home, their cars and their staunch pride. Years later, when I was pouring through our household paperwork, I found my father's W–2, which stated his annual income. My eyes welled up with tears of gratitude and quite honestly, a fistful of anger because he had been unable to follow his true and more lucrative passion of being a commercial pilot. I literally couldn't understand how they did it. My mother, Margaret Coleman, used to always say as a stay–at–home mom, she could make a nickel "holler."

From high school to this day, I have worked, invested and saved. Having my own money gave me a sense of freedom to choose how I would spend my extra funds and how I would save my money for larger purchases. I also longed for more–more education, more culture, more adventure and more ownership.

I realized the power that financial freedom brings. Throughout college, business school and my entire career, I devised a plan to pursue only appreciable assets. While my parents were frugal, they also sought appreciation and steered away from the normal staples of perceived success. We had one 1969 Oldsmobile 98 that resembled Das Boot, which we kept until it died, and a 1966 Ford Mustang, which my younger brother still owns. On the other hand, the home my parents purchased for less than $30,000 in the 70s sold for $540,000 in 2019. Sadly, my mother sold after my father passed, yet with this prudent investment, she reaped six times the purchase price. The proceeds sustained her until her early death.

Except for the occasional "retail blackout moment," I've always been fairly strict about my savings plan. One reason was a life–altering insight I gained in my HBS Organizational Behavior class.

Everyone snapped to attention when my HBS professor told the class we should all have an account with "F–you money." Today, it's called "walk away money" or "FIRE" (Financial Independence Retire Early).

Throughout my career, I've stayed closest to departments in which the economic value for the company is derived. When you control the money, either personally or within a corporation, you have greater power and flexibility. Money gives you the cushion to try new things.

I've co–founded two companies, left two companies and returned to the same company only to leave for another post–IPO company. Not all were financial windfalls, but enough were to balance out the risk portfolio. In some cases, you could say, "I'm funny about my money," but through delayed gratification, a structured combination of real estate, stock equity and P&L responsibility, I feel abundant.

Having an HBS, Wharton trained, CFA husband also helps. We call ourselves Team Stewart as the blending of our skills makes for a powerful partnership.

Today I am elevating my focus by taking my investments to the next level and finding my voice at the "cap table" with early and mid–stage investments.

Jackie–Having Enough

I have always had enough, even when I have had to redefine just what "enough" meant. I began to understand the value of money and real estate quite early.

My parents were hardworking and middle class. They bought a three–decker home in the Roxbury section of Boston when I was in elementary school. We lived on the second and part of the third floors. We had renters on the first and third floors. My father worked two jobs throughout my childhood. He was a licensed practical nurse at a Boston hospital and worked the overnight shift. In the mornings, he drove to a suburban dry cleaner to earn a second salary. When I was in nursery school, my mother, Louise Adams, returned to the workforce as an assistant teacher at the school. She began a career as a psychiatric social worker when I was in high school.

As I wrote in Chapter One, my father took his role as a provider very seriously. He wouldn't let me babysit. He didn't want me to take care of somebody else's kids. In fact, he protected me from a good bit of household work.

My first paying job in high school was in my chosen field. I worked for the newspaper, The Christian Science Monitor. I started in the circulation department and quickly moved up to become a "copy kid" in the newsroom, interacting with reporters and editors.

At age 22, I signed my first contract for my first job as a broadcaster. I remember being struck by the fact that my first job out of college paid me more than twice the joint income that my parents had reported on the financial aid forms that I submitted as an incoming freshman. Within 18 months, I paid off my college loans.

Within three years, at age 25, I bought my first condominium on Boston's tony Beacon Street. I loved that apartment. It was technically a one–bedroom, but it had a lovely nook with doors and a window seat that I used as an office. The apartment had two fireplaces, a breathtaking view of the Charles River, and it was within earshot of Boston Pops concerts at the famous Hatch Shell. I still use the barstools I bought for that kitchen's island. It's true that real estate can be a basis for wealth creation. After three *years, I sold that apartment, made a 25% profit and used those funds to buy and sell subsequent homes in Washington, D.C., and New York City.*

When I decided to leave CBS News after 22 years, I decided that "freedom was not free" and took a significant pay cut. But then and now, I've always had enough.

I have always been pretty Zen about money. I admit my attitude has been a bit of a luxury. I admit I haven't amassed the wealth that a lot of my HBS classmates have. My strategy has been to take every preparatory step you can think of — and then, "be still and know."

Psalm 46:10 says: "Be still, and know that I am God; I will be exalted among the nations, I will be exalted in the earth." For me, that means be patient and let knowledge and goodness come to you. Your serenity conveys, especially to yourself, supreme confidence, and you are then exalted.

It is prudent to have backup plans A, B and C, of course. The knowledge that you have genuine, realistic and personally acceptable options available to you lessens your fear and bolsters your confidence. And I believe in what Amazon CEO Jeff Bezos has said: "If you can make a decision with analysis, you should do so. But it turns out in life that your most important decisions are always made with instinct and intuition."

It's important to realize cash is not the only currency. Connections, friendships, people—otherwise known as networking—can also convey power. They also convey influence.

The man who gave me my first job after CBS News also gave me great advice: "Take everyone you know out to lunch and join everything you can join." That bit of wisdom has served me well in my second career, my entrepreneurial career.

I am something of a "connector." I hear and remember people's skills, desires, needs. I consider these all to be "dots." My favorite activity is aligning those "dots" – turning them into lines. It makes people happy, and when they pay me for assisting with this alignment, they pay me well.

Networking gets a bad rap. Yes, you do want people with whom you network to do something FOR you, but they are more likely to respond if you FIRST do something for them. The essence of networking is service. Even if that service is only sending a thank you note, people remember those gestures and, in my experience, they respond in kind.

A final thought about money comes from the Billie Holiday song, "God bless the child that's got his own." As I've written, my father didn't believe in following clothing fads. That philosophy was fine until I was about 16 and mohair sweaters became all the rage.

I recall staging a full–blown fit in the major department store in Boston to get a mohair sweater. And I succeeded! But, like Scarlett O'Hara holding up that turnip in the classic movie, Gone with the Wind, *I vowed I would never humiliate myself ever again to get something I really wanted. Metaphorically, I would never go hungry again!*

And I never have. I have worked, saved and bought every sweater I even thought I wanted.

Paula and Jackie—Money

I don't like calling Paula (not her real name) my "oldest" friend. We met when we were assigned as roommates when we studied Shakespeare at Oxford University during a summer program between our junior and senior years in college. Instead, I call her my "friend of longest standing."

A lifelong friendship, especially among women, is a blessing. We attended each other's weddings and have shared each other's joys and sorrows. I have always been in awe of her dynamism, her courage and humor, as well as the uniqueness of her Pacific Island heritage.

Paula was the first of my friends to become a self–made millionaire. An admitted risk–taker, she bought a seat on one of the commodity exchanges before she turned 30. Although she was and remains quite level headed, she once told me about a particularly good trading day. How good? With one day's earnings, she was able to make an admittedly extravagant purchase, her first sports car. Grateful for her success, she made a major donation to her college, enabling the school to launch its women's studies department. She was cited as the youngest major donor in her state university's history.

Paula started a second career in real estate in her 50s and again, made an excellent return developing properties in and around Boston.

There was very little wealth in her childhood, but she worked incredibly hard. She entered a brutally competitive field, especially for women, but it was also an industry that rewarded performance and competence.

Who better, I thought, to ask about wealth creation? I got an earful!

Building wealth now is a myth! I don't even like that word "wealth." Today it's primarily associated with the phrase "wealth disparities."

Instead, let's talk about money. But before we do, I want to stress three things:

- *The best investment is in your health; this should be your number one priority.*
- *You must exercise, rest and sleep.*
- *Time is your number one asset. You never have as much as you need and it's a luxury to spend time with your family and friends.*

The subject of money is pretty straightforward. If you have some, you have no need to worry. Money should give you freedom — freedom to pursue your passions like painting or travel.

Look at the various asset classes: real estate, stocks, bonds, mutual funds, commodities, gold and other metals, the dollar. The risks and prices of all of them today make them out of reach for most young people, especially those burdened with huge amounts of student debt.

I have great compassion for young people because it's appalling that their best source of security now is their friends and families. It's not going to come from corporate management.

Long–term prosperity is the result of your income and savings and those come from having a good job. However, productivity is flat or at zero. There are only so many extra dollars most young people will have access to for savings. In Europe, many banks are now charging you to protect your money. With negative interest rates, you deposit $100 and they give you back $99. I can see the practice of putting money under your mattress on the horizon here in the U.S. It may become your safest option!

The dollar has been secure, but given our burgeoning federal debt, I'm not sure about the long–term safety of the dollar. When will foreigners abandon U.S. treasuries? I could see it happening.

Pensions are a thing of the past. Corporations don't want to be liable for defined pension benefits, but who can put aside enough money to make IRAs a meaningful retirement cushion.

Housing had been the best avenue for building wealth for 90% of Americans, but that's been taken away. Real estate is no longer the affordable asset it was for you and me. Prices everywhere across the country are ridiculously high and in 2017, Congress eliminated the last tax protections for most real estate. Deductions for all state and local property, income and sales taxes are now capped at just $10,000.

Climate change is destroying wealth. Think about the droughts, wildfires and hurricanes that have destroyed acres and acres of land and hard assets. Insurers are going broke paying for the damage. Weren't there $22 billion in losses in 14 major storms in the first nine months of 2019?

For women, choosing whom you marry is as important as which asset class you select. That second income can be a major boost — or a major drag — on your financial status.

I went from being a happy English major to being a commodity and bond trader. Later, I chose real estate. My choices always reflected my tolerance for risk. A critical component of those choices was working for bosses who looked out for me.

You have to think about your education because you might need specialized education to grow in the job/career of your choosing. If I were doing it all again, I'd choose a career that can't be automated, a career that requires the human touch, a job in which you go eyeball–to–eyeball. Those human relationships are always the keys to success. Today, most of the trading is done by computers. There's no competitive edge when you're working against a silent machine.

I tell young people to forget about magical thinking. Get off your phones! The internet is a drug! Go out and walk to get your dinner instead of having it delivered to you. Put aside the money you're spending on apps that turn your photos into dancing pigs. Study history! Get involved in your communities! Work together with your friends! Go out and vote!

We all have a responsibility to participate in the search for solutions. But none of them is going to be easy.

Prison Muscles and Freedom

Whenever the conversation turns to finance, some of us might have more modest aspirations. Perhaps the goal shouldn't be money or wealth. Perhaps we should choose another word, something like "comfort."

Whatever we call it, we all want more. And many of us can acquire more. The pool of African American future leaders, especially women leaders, is growing with our increases in those completing college educations and advanced degrees. Corporations are increasingly looking for those leaders, as the financial and productivity benefits of diverse workforces become more widely understood. The numbers of Black female entrepreneurs are also spiking.

But Harvard Business School alum, retired professor Steven Rogers, worries that business leaders of color work only on what he calls their "prison muscles." They bulk up in areas like marketing and communications, like inmates bulking up only their upper bodies, because muscle development of the legs is harder work and the results of the work are covered by long pants. Unfortunately, many Black business leaders do the same partial body muscle development, instead of becoming complete business athletes with equally strong financial expertise.

To combat this imbalance, Rogers has developed a three-hour seminar on Entrepreneurial Finance, which he is delivering on the campuses of Historically Black Colleges and Universities, as well as in the poorest communities in Chicago, his hometown. Financed by John Rogers and Mellody Hobson of Ariel Capital, professor Rogers has been teaching young Black entrepreneurs about key financial concepts, such as a company's internal rate of return, return on investments, debt and equity financing, and the methodology for an entrepreneur to determine how much money he needs. He covers the fundamentals of finance, valuation models, access to capital, cost of capital and other topics essential to becoming a successful entrepreneur.

As Rogers has written, "Research shows that less than two percent of all equity capital and five percent of Small Business Administration (SBA) debt capital was invested in Black entrepreneurs last year. As one Black entrepreneur stated, 'We have a better chance of raising capital by playing the lottery.'" His course is an effort to improve the odds of capital raising, that results in the increase in job and wealth creation in the Black community.

And what goes hand in hand with power and influence is freedom—particularly financial independence and wealth creation.

In the spring of 2019, Jackie took a Juilliard Evening Division course on The Freedom Sound: Jazz in the Turbulent 60s. On the final day, she asked Professor Reggie Quinerly to define the freedom sound. He quoted pianist/singer/composer

Nina Simone: "The freedom sound is no fear! No fear to be yourself or of repercussions from what they will think or of the beauty rules. The freedom sound is self–expression."

For Bonita, Nina Simone's words, delivered at her father's funeral, say it all: "If I found I could fly, I'd soar to the sun."

 **LIVING LOG**

- ❑ What are you worth? How do you measure your worth?
- ❑ Do you have shortterm and long–term money goals?
- ❑ Do you whisper about money or actively seek to improve your financial literacy?
- ❑ How do you align your self–worth with that which your environment values?
- ❑ Build a nest egg early in your career and focus on appreciable assets. Equities and real estate are good places to start.
- ❑ Are you building wealth for financial independence?
- ❑ Are you prepared for a financial catastrophe — an illness or a job loss?
- ❑ Are you investing in appreciable asset categories?
- ❑ Become a natural entrepreneur and intrapreneur.
- ❑ Learn to know how and when to exercise delayed gratification.
- ❑ Keep your own "gotta go" fund.
- ❑ Understand the power of building wealth vs. collecting things.

Chapter Three

Onward Sole Sisters

W hen we began developing the themes for this book, we knew an important one would be the intersection of "being an only," i.e., racial and gender isolation or loneliness in the workplace and stress.

During our educations and careers, we and scores of our fellow Harvard Business School alumnae have experienced this stress, tried to manage it or worked overtime to ignore it. The typical remedies have been exercise or medical care for various stress–related illnesses or that old favorite, toughing it out. Prayer has been another option.

Over the last few years, the amount of research on stress, from myriad perspectives, has been eye–popping. Studies have described in detail the manifestations of "only–ness" and found that it exacts an "emotional tax" that is genuinely hazardous to the health of women of color. Researchers have looked at women of color in business, law and medicine, among other fields. The stress of being a college student of color is now being studied, and in the popular media, we see stories and films about the impact of stress in entertainment as well as in the music and sports industries. There are also books and research on the benefits of white privilege. For us, seeing the flip side of the race–based stresses we have experienced was chilling.

The most recent Census Bureau data from 2013 sets the table.[39]

- Black women are 51% of the Black population in the U.S.;
- 71% of Black women, aged 16–64, are in the labor force versus 69% of all women;
- Yet 29% of Black women are below the poverty level versus 17% for all women;
- 64% of Black women hold white–collar jobs (defined as management, business, computers, office, legal and education) versus 72% of all women;
- 48% of Black women have never married versus 30% of all women;
- Only 26% of Black women are currently married versus 46% of all women;
- 33% of Black women gave birth while married versus 64% of all women;
- 13% of Black women are divorced versus 3% of all women;
- Yet 364,000 more Black men are married than Black women;
- The median earnings of Black women are $38,780 versus $38,097 for all women.

Yes, more Black women in the U.S. are in the workforce, in white–collar jobs, earning a slightly higher median salary. But more of us are parenting alone and must rely on just one salary more than all women. Sometimes you're stressed because you're under stress! Not being able to express your anger about these facts, experts say, can increase your exhaustion and stress.

New studies lay the origins of stress–related health issues among African Americans to the legacy of slavery. At an October 2019 Harvard conference, the Dean of the T.H. Chan School of Public Health, Michelle A. Williams, reported that the United States is one of only 13 countries in the world where more women die in childbirth today than they did 25 years ago and African American women are three to four times more likely to die than whites.

As reported in the *Harvard Gazette*, Dean Williams said a Black woman with an advanced degree is more likely to lose her baby than a white woman with an eighth–grade education. Worse, certain stereotypes with roots in slavery have endured to the present—notably the idea that Black people do not feel pain in the same way whites do, a notion once used to justify whipping and other abuse.

"This has wormed its way into scientific theory and a study published in 2016–yes, 2016–said a majority of medical students still believe it." This makes being Black a risk factor in itself, she said.[40]

Stress is high for all women at work, especially Millennials.

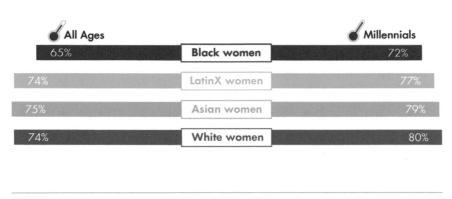

All Ages		Millennials
65%	Black women	72%
74%	LatinX women	77%
75%	Asian women	79%
74%	White women	80%

Women of Color in Business: Cross Generational Survey©

Indeed, in our proprietary *Women of Color in Business: Cross Generational Survey©*, women knowledge workers across all races report extraordinarily high levels of stress on the job. Sadly, the percentages are even higher for the youngest workers among us, with 80 percent of white Millennial women topping this unenviable chart. Although the numbers for Black women across the generations are high, it is interesting that we are either managing our stress somewhat better or we are just, yet again, "making a way out of no way." It could also be that the stress is manifesting itself in ways we don't even fully recognize.

Even our beauty treatments may be harming us. A new study published by the *International Journal of Cancer* found that "Black women who regularly used permanent dyes to color their hair were 60 percent more likely to develop breast cancer, compared to Black women who did not report using dye." The report continues that white women using hair dye did not see an increased risk. The study also found that those women of all races who used hair straighteners had a 30% increase in the risk of breast cancer.[41]

In our analysis of all the data, our bottom line is that there is a "myth of inferiority" against which women and men of color are forced to battle every day and in every aspect of life. Furthermore, the evidence shows that battle is exacting tremendous physical and psychological costs. Nonetheless, as we and countless others have demonstrated, we are facing just a myth, and this knowledge alone should help us defuse/deactivate its power. Shattering that myth of inferiority, examining our pain, sharing our stories and teaming up to celebrate our strengths are among the antidotes that have animated our writing this book.

Buckle up.

Being "An Only" in Corporations

Until the last decade or so, being an "only" and its impact on workplace stress had been a theory, a feeling, perhaps even an urban myth. Increasingly, research is showing not only that "only–ness" in the corporate world has costs, but that those costs are profound. Let's look at the data.

One of our fellow HBS African American alumnae is Dame Vivian Hunt, the managing partner at McKinsey & Company U.K. and Ireland. She reports that currently, only 79 women are promoted to manager for every 100 men. Gender or racial equity in the workplace is decades away, even though the companies in her survey say they are genuinely trying.

In the meantime, women of color continue to plug along. Using data from 279 companies employing more than 13 million people as well as surveys of more than 64,000 workers, McKinsey & Company's *Women in the Workplace 2018* study confirmed that for more than three decades, women have been:

- earning more bachelor's degrees than men;
- asking for promotions and negotiating salaries at the same rates as men; and,
- contrary to conventional wisdom, they are staying in the workforce at the same rate as men.

Yet, corporate America has made almost no progress in improving women's representation since the first study in 2015. Notably, "women of color are the most underrepresented group of all, lagging behind white men, men of color, and white women."[42]

The results of this underrepresentation are significant. McKinsey found that women of color report many more instances of major microaggressions over the course of their careers, including:

- Having your judgment questioned in your area of expertise;
- Needing to provide more evidence of your competence than others do;
- Being addressed in a less than professional manner;
- Being mistaken for someone at a much lower level than you are;
- Hearing demeaning remarks about you or people like you.

The results complement the findings of Roberts, Mayo and Thomas in *Race, Work & Leadership* that Black workers report lower levels of engagement than non–black respondents, including:

- Less perceived importance of their role in light of the mission or purpose of the company;
- Fewer opportunities to learn and grow in the past year;
- Lower levels of overall satisfaction with the workplace.

Perhaps more damning was the research documenting the challenges Black leaders face in establishing credibility and taking charge, among them:

- Deficit–based thinking that associates blackness with disadvantage, risk, unintelligence and disinterest in challenging and complex intellectual tasks;
- Implicit biases that lead people to doubt the legitimacy and credibility of Black (and other non–prototypical) leaders, and to fear those Black leaders who exercise authoritative leadership.[43]

The think tank, Catalyst, now reports that the bias–generated stresses that men and especially women of color face in the workplaces are hazardous to their health. A 2018 survey of some 1,600 professionals in business and the nonprofit, education and government sectors called the impact an "emotional tax," one that particularly affects women of color.

"Women of color continue to deal with some of the workplace's most entrenched hurdles such as pay inequities and near invisibility in top leadership roles, as well as daunting roadblocks that stifle the meaningful dialogue that would help make real progress," said Dnika J. Travis, vice president, research at Catalyst.

How does this "emotional tax" manifest itself? Travis said Asian women (51%), Black women (58%), Latina (56%) and multiracial women (52%) report they feel "highly on guard," and as a result, women of color believe they must outwork and outperform their colleagues. Yet, the report found that "despite being on guard, nearly all women of color want to be influential leaders. Ninety percent want to have challenging and intellectually stimulating work, obtain high–ranking positions and stay at the same company."[44]

The Cost of Perfection

Several of our Harvard colleagues privately shared stories about the toxicity of the stresses they have endured at work, some self–inflicted and some caused by co–workers. But the pain of those experiences remains so searing, so fresh, especially in our new #MeToo era, none wanted details to be reported here, even if their identities were disguised. We are complying with their wishes, but we encourage our readers to inventory the circumstances in which their health, both physical and mental, may have been compromised in an effort to be tough, to go above and beyond, to be a "superwoman."

Zuhairah's Story—Squeezing Joy into Your Day

Zuhairah Scott Washington wrote movingly about the "home" she feels within the African American community at Harvard Business School. In her AASU50 profile[45], she called it a "place where I feel accepted, fed, and stretched, all at the same time. Having that sense of 'home,' especially when working in industries not used to seeing folks who look like me in leadership positions, is fundamental to my success as a Black female tech executive."

Zuhairah is carrying a heavy load. She has two young sons, a new baby daughter, a husband with whom she regularly strives to have dinner alone and a big job that involves lots of international travel as Senior Vice President for strategic global partnerships for a Fortune 500 travel technology company. She admits she does face stress, but she is both philosophical and practical about coping with it. "A benefit of having a childhood that wasn't always rosy is that you cope with stress early. I'm not easily blown off my rocker. My resilience makes me effective. It takes a lot of discontent to really stress me out."

Zuhairah lists several tactics she uses to "make space to recalibrate." She calls it intentional turning off: "reading, writing, sitting and chatting with my five–year–old about Legos, going into his world rather than being obsessed with mine, finding joy in my sons' lives." She added that since she can often work from home, she deliberately sets aside time for her seven–year–old. "He would come home from school excited to see me and strike up a conversation and I'd be locked in my office on a conference call. So, one day, I just made him my 3:30 p.m. meeting. I've had to be intentional about it. But I told myself that I would block off this time for him, just so that we can talk and check–in on his day."

Being "An Only" in Medicine

The stress of being "an only "doesn't impact only women of color in business. As we have written, we have discovered numerous new studies, research, reporting and data on the topic, assessing women of color in medicine, law and fields that include theology and academia. If the results all sound similar, it's because they are.

Medical student and reporter Jessica Yang assembled some of the statistics and findings for the website, Zora. She wrote: "Women physicians face constant reminders that they are women in a field created by males, that no matter what they say or how they dress, that they will be mistaken to be everyone except for the physician. Being a person of color in medicine comes with its own issues—from lack of mentorship and guidance to the complexities of applying to medical school and navigating the bureaucracies."

Yang added that women's experiences do not get better once the already small population of women of color trainees reach positions within academic medicine.

- Women of color make up just 3.2% of full professor positions in the field.
- Women who are non–white and clinical faculty members leave full–time appointments at higher rates than white men who are basic science faculty.
- Many cite issues of discrimination, institutional road-blocks, bias, lack of mentorship and more as reasons for leaving.

Further, women of color are disproportionately selected to sit on diversity focus groups and committees, which takes time away from their scholarly pursuits, which are necessary to advance in academia. Yang's conclusion: "This 'minority' tax can lead to burnout and additional frustrations, further exacerbating the lack of women of color in academic positions."

Yang quoted Uche Blackstock, M.D., an emergency medicine physician and Chief Executive Officer of Advancing Health Equity, who said there is an added burden for women of color who are in a jeopardy situation—speaking up means risking the negative stereotype of being an aggressive minority, while not speaking up can lead to assumptions that they are not assertive enough.[46]

Bonita's Story—The Burden & The Joy

Women of color count twice, but we have the burden (or joy, depending on your perspective) of having to contribute twice as much. Routinely, we are volunteering time and brainpower to support our company's employee resource groups as well as minority associations. In effect, we are asked to do more than one job at a time.

*As a faith–based person, I take Luke 12:48 seriously: "For unto whomsoever **much is given**, of him/her shall be **much** required." Indeed, the joy should be ours to bring others along and to welcome the limelight that accompanies being the role model whom so many desperately crave. Here are several tactics I've come to employ:*

I established open office hours for anyone in the company to have 15 minutes of one–on–one time with me. The short time frame forces succinctness, and it's amazing what can happen in 15 minutes. You can meet someone new, coach someone in a tough situation, hear a new idea or simply provide your wisdom on "What would Bonita do?"

Over the years, I've tried to reduce the burden and stress of the role model role by giving others leadership practice. I believe that when you are standing in the sun, you should share your sunshine with others. While I do feel an obligation to be in the spotlight, I am mastering the art of saying: "No. However, I have someone you should meet." The day when you become tired of being tired, you must pass the baton–often.

I have so many inbound requests for speaking engagements or other invitations, I am known as "high traffic." I often take these opportunities to recommend another woman "rock star" to take my place. Recently, when I was asked to host a panel on leadership, I brought along two of my amazing leaders to share the panel with me.

Women of color must be allowed to do their "day job" without the full burden of extracurricular activities we know are essential to sharing our success with others. I've often thought male allies could and should share this responsibility and every now and then, they surprise me. During one meeting, I took a deep breath and smiled when a fellow executive said the career development burden should not be isolated to the under–represented minorities to advance but should be shared by everyone.

Stresses in the Legal Profession

In the new book, *Race, Work & Leadership*, Harvard Law School Professor David B. Wilkins and HLS Lecturer Bryan Fong examined *Intersectionality and the Careers of Black Women Lawyers.*[47] Specifically, they looked at the significance of race and gender in the careers of Black graduates of the school, with a focus on those who graduated from 2000 τo 2016. The authors note that their data includes former President Barack Obama as well as his wife, former First Lady Michelle Obama.

86

First, the good news: considerable progress has been made in that the majority of minority law students are women at Harvard, as well as at virtually every law school in the country. And sisters in law, as they sometimes call themselves, are racking up significant victories.

In Houston's Harris County, the third–largest county in America dubbed the epicenter of mass incarceration, 19 Black women won their races for judgeships in November 2018. They campaigned together under the slogan "Black Girl Magic," and their election reflects the increase in women of color running in and winning local, state and (perhaps soon) national races.[48]

The Houston victories followed the election of nine Black women judges in Jefferson County, Alabama in 2016. There, Circuit Court Domestic Relations Judge Nakita Blocton has no illusions about the influence she has on her community. She has said: "Lawyers and judges are like doctors. We're powerful. We can take your children away. We can take your house away, take your car away. We touch people's lives in an extraordinary way, and that is a huge duty." Circuit Civil Court Judge Tamara Harris Johnson added: "As an African American woman, I have a responsibility to make sure that people not only respect my intelligence but respect my work. All of us want the same things; we want life, liberty and the pursuit of happiness. I don't want the hatred. I don't want the racism. So whatever I can do to help that, I'll do."[49]

But here's the bad news. The Wilkins–Fong research found that Black Harvard Law School graduates, especially Black women, are consistently less satisfied with many aspects of their careers, experience worse career outcomes than Black men and are less likely to recommend a law degree to a young person.

Black women are starting their careers in the largest law firms at higher rates than Black men. However, over time, both male and female Black HLS graduates leave private practice at much higher rates than white and Black lawyers nationally, with females more likely to go into public interest law or education.

Between 2005 and 2016, the average Black partnership rate was just 1.7% with a peak of 1.81% in 2016. Yet, in 2016, African American women constituted just 0.64% of all partners, and they reported being even less satisfied with their private practice careers than their Black male peers.

Bonita's Story—At the Ballet

When people refer to my leadership style, they commonly use the word "grace" or "grace under fire." I can understand why, because I have always worked to manifest grace physically.

From a very early age, I loved dance—tap, ballet, jazz, modern. I tried them all, and I settled on ballet. It was strenuous yet regal. While I had some early opportunities to dance as an extra with the Cleo Parker Robinson Dance Ensemble and the Joyce Little Dancers in Denver where I grew up, I was never on the professional track.

After not being selected for a dance audition during junior high school, my father was a warm balm of comfort as the rejection pierced my pride. He responded by offering me the best advice one could imagine. He encouraged me to take my love for dance and carry it with me forever as a hobby while combining it with my academic achievement.

Little did I know, ballet would become my sacred space where I could retreat, wash away sorrow, release anger and find liberation.

A Chorus Line debuted on Broadway in 1975. One of the show's songs, "At the Ballet," became MY song because it seemed "everything was beautiful at the ballet." The words of the song became my business affirmation. And my interpretation became: Everyone is worthy.

Although I was still usually one of just a handful of women of color in the class, ballet became and still is my lifelong hobby and stress reducer. Happily, diversity has made its way into the dance world. I have moved from pink tights and shoes to caramel tights and shoes over the years.

The studio became my hidden sanctuary. The studio became another learning lab for leadership. Ballet combines discipline, collaboration, problem–solving, complexity, failing and trying again and again. Nothing beats nailing the perfect pirouette or an explosive jete for joy.

Throughout my academic training and work career, I would always find my respite in the ballet studio surrounded by soothing classical music, like–minded women, a barre and four walls of freedom.

Stress and Students of Color

Bonita found that ballet was an effective stress–reducer in high school, college and beyond. But studies indicate her experience is not typical among today's students of color.

A 2015 Harris Poll of 1,502 students, ages 17 to 20, found that 51% of African American college students felt "overwhelmed most or all of the time." Unfortunately, Black and

Hispanic students are more likely to keep their distress to themselves.[50]

Their symptoms include depression, anxiety and even increased risk for suicide. Experts find that students of color receive care for their mental health needs much less often than white students. The cause for this deficit has less to do with money, insurance or access and more with "psycho–social barriers" or an internal "self–stigma" that keeps people of color from seeking care.

"This speaks to the fact that Black folks have been talking about this pain and suffering for a long time now, and the typical response is 'It's all in your head,' or 'You need to suck it up,' said Ebony McGee, a researcher at Vanderbilt University's Peabody College who has studied Black students' mental health concerns.

At the Ballet–Part Two

From the outside, American Ballet Theater principal dancer Misty Copeland is a perfect exemplar of excellence with success, beauty, athleticism and lucrative endorsements that are atypical in the dance world.

She is the first woman of color to be selected in the company's 75–year history, and her selection landed her on the cover of *Time Magazine*. Nonetheless, in her first commercial for her line of Under Armour athletic wear, her tagline was defiant and defensive: "I will what I want."

In just 30 seconds, Copeland gave voice to the psychological pain that too often afflicts girls and women of color: rejection. "Like many women, I was told that I wasn't good enough and that I couldn't succeed, but I willed myself to where I am now. I think that's a message that resonates with all women. Success isn't handed to us: we earn it."[51]

In 2014, Bonita fulfilled a promise to herself. Jackie was thrilled to have been included.

I saw Misty Copeland as a "sister." I shared her love for dance and knew in my toes how difficult her path had been. Anticipating that she would become the first African American principal ballerina at American Ballet Theatre, (ABT) I brought 14 African American women to her debut in the role of ABT's Swanilda in the George Balanchine classic, Coppelia. *In a fiercely competitive art form, she rose to perfection, and that night, she danced her heart out.*

My version of support is sitting front and center, standing and cheering "Brava, Brava." I wanted Misty as well as the largely white Lincoln Center audience to see my posse of women of color cheering her on. We filled almost an entire row in the orchestra, and in fact, I did notice a few raised eyebrows from some in the audience. Until Misty became a superstar, not many African Americans had frequented ABT performances.

As a patron donor of ABT, I was able to treat my friends to champagne during intermission and to bring them backstage after the performance. As exciting as it was to watch Misty on stage, it was even more meaningful to see her tears as she accepted our love and gratitude in person. She had earned her success, and we were all happy to share in it.

All of us had been the "first" African American woman in some or other situation. All of us had endured stresses from the loneliness of our only–ness. Dance and choreography had always been my passions, and I knew firsthand how lonely the spotlight can be. I swore to myself I would always fight for the pioneers and

91

those who dared to break boundaries, especially within the Black community. I swore to myself I would invite other women of color to join me in that fight. On that one night—at the ballet—we shared a collective victory.

Black Pain

Businesswoman and author Terrie Williams coped with emotional stress the way most women of color did and still do. She didn't seek care; she just soldiered on until one day, she couldn't get out of bed. As she began to heal herself, she vowed to help others. A decade ago, she wrote a groundbreaking book, *Black Pain: It Just Looks Like We're Not Hurting.*

Jackie first came to know Terrie as the public relations executive for *Essence* magazine. She also represented a number of hugely successful African American music and movie stars. Terrie was kind and astute enough to hand-write a lovely congratulations note when she read about Jackie's 1989 marriage to *New York Times* correspondent, Gerald M. Boyd.

More recently, Jackie has heard Terrie speak about her battle with depression and the epidemic of untreated clinical depression in the Black community. Terrie has said: "We self–soothe our emotional and psychological wounds through eating disorders, drug and alcohol abuse, working 24/7, excessive gambling or shopping, promiscuous sex, hiding from the world, and more violence and crime. What must happen is that we must finally come out of the shadows of our depression, speak about it, and get professional help that addresses our root trauma."

Say what? Working 24/7 and shopping are forms of self–soothing? Working 24/7 and shopping might be symptoms of depression? Jackie was an expert at both of those techniques, but had never considered either to be symptoms of her pain.

Terrie continued: "I wrote the book as a way to show us ourselves through the mirror of shared feelings, thoughts, and experiences reflected by practically every walk of life–from the corporate executive to our youth, our moms and men, to gang bangers–so that we recognize what depression looks, sounds, and feels like in plain English."

Terrie's goal dovetails with ours—that people of color, especially women of color, don't have to continue suffering alone or in silence. She added: "My goal for *Black Pain* is to empower us to do the real work necessary to heal and move forward in a whole, healthy life, to free ourselves from the bondage of depressive disorders. But it all starts with admitting that we have a problem and speaking honestly about it."[52]

Jackie's Story—Turning Myself Inside Out

"How do you comfort yourself?"

What a strange question, *I thought. I didn't have an answer to this first question the psychiatrist asked me in our first counseling session.*

I had been under extreme stress at work for decades. After all, daily or even hourly deadlines were givens. I had never considered being a woman of color, often the "only" woman of color in any or most circumstances, as an additional element of my professional stress. The stresses for the men, of any color, but especially for the white men, were the same—almost. They could be mediocre, but I couldn't.

The most damning sin was not making your "slot" in the next broadcast, which meant completing the reporting, organizing and writing of your story in time to give your co–workers sufficient time to do their work. They included producers and executive producers who reviewed and approved the scripts and then the all–important videotape editors, who polished the stories visually. Think of it as an assembly line. Everything was a team effort, but my job as the correspondent was the first domino that had to fall. I accepted the stress and came to think of it as a version of the old game show, Beat the Clock. *In almost 30 years, I don't recall ever having missed my slot. And I was proud of that accomplishment.*

One of my best/worst days was when my crew and I landed in Dayton, Ohio, at 2 p.m. to report on an auto strike. We did all of our work in time to lead the 6:30 p.m. evening broadcast. Four and a half hours–soup to nuts: reporting, interviewing, writing, getting approvals, recording the narration and videotaping my on camera standup, editing and transmitting by satellite – no problem!

But of course, the stress found an outlet. At various times, I experienced hives and hypersensitivity on my hands and arms. Happily, I found that a mild antihistamine and/or diuretic kept the welts at bay and thank goodness, the stress never showed up on the skin on my face, scalp or neck.

The reason I finally saw a psychiatrist was because the additional stress of enduring and ultimately ending an unhappy marriage to a very demanding husband pushed me over the edge. Only recently have I come to understand his stresses as "an only" – as one of the highest–ranking African American men in a largely white corporation. His childhood, far more volatile and deprived than mine, left him more vulnerable to untreated clinical depression. It was a subject I didn't understand at the time.

Early in our relationship, I had begun to projectile vomit, mostly in hotels when I was traveling for work. But as the marriage came closer to an end, I couldn't keep much in my stomach at home. At one point, there was so much food in the drains in my bathroom that I had to call an exterminator to deal with fruit flies. The psychiatrist theorized I was trying to turn myself inside out—literally—to make the marriage work. Once my husband moved out for good, I stopped throwing up, and I haven't thrown up since.

"How do you comfort yourself?"

I didn't.

Recently, I have come to realize I coped with most of the professional stress by going numb. It was the only way to achieve the SuperGirl image I had for myself. I scrupulously avoided the lows but didn't allow myself many genuine highs.

I couldn't tell you what I believed politically—while I was covering national politics—because my job was to see all sides of every issue and report them dispassionately, fairly. I avoided movies or books that dealt with slavery or Jim Crow because I knew they would make me angry and sad, and I had no way to process those feelings, no safe place to put those feelings. I couldn't allow myself to feel justifiable rage.

Today, of course, going numb or projectile vomiting or taking antihistamines would not be considered healthy options. I did begin going to the gym during my divorce and was thrilled to discover, however belatedly, that exercise is an effective form of stress reduction.

More recently, I have been fascinated to learn that there are studies about "authenticity tension" and "facades of conformity" and "workplace satisfaction."

It seems almost quaint that my laser focus didn't contemplate authenticity or the costs of conformity. I focused on earning a good salary, doing work I mostly considered fun, and trying to project an image of excellence on the nation's airwaves. Who knew there could be more–for me personally, for my mental health, for my former husband, for my "comfort?" Could I have achieved even more if I had dropped my Supergirl cape and found ways to ease what I now recognize as pain?

Dr. Modupe Akinola —We Are Enough!

Dr. Modupe Akinola earned her MBA and Ph.D. at Harvard Business School and is now a tenured professor at Columbia Business School. She is one of a growing cadre of African American academics, many of them female, whose research into various aspects of diversity and stress is being published in academic journals and practitioner–oriented outlets.

Modupe is an expert on the effects of stress on performance as well as the biases that affect the recruitment and retention of minorities in organizations. She examines these topics using experimental methodologies, including physiological responses (specifically hormonal and cardiovascular responses), behavioral observation, and implicit and reaction time measures.

She worries there is a misperception about the nature of stress. On the one hand, stress can be debilitating, hindering performance. This she knows firsthand. While she was studying for her Ph.D., she underwent a physical assessment at her gym and learned her body age was four years older than her actual age of 33! Modupe turned to running to relieve her stress, which had a positive effect on her studies, and in 2018, she completed her first marathon.

However, much of Modupe's research also shows that stress can be enhancing, preparing the body and mind for action and performance, which she often experiences.

Modupe has been gratified that her research on stress has had an impact on the academic community and that this impact is expanding to organizations and the general public. She is particularly interested in the role stress plays in communities of color. For instance, what are the unique stressors that affect MBA students of color and their career trajectories? What are the extra stressors faced by women of color at work, who juggle numerous obligations inside and outside of the office? She has recognized that some of this stress comes from people feeling as if they aren't enough.

My goal is to help leaders, especially women, realize that they are enough. One more accomplishment won't lead to greater happiness. We are good enough as we are and need to do deep introspective work to understand the dysfunctions that have been passed down, leading to this belief of "not being enough." This introspection will have a ripple effect. Men need us to be enlightened so that they can know that they are enough, collectively, ending the cycle of transmitting these insecurities to future generations.

Modupe's research echoes the lived experience of one of Jackie's HBS classmates, a single mother whose spectacularly successful career required weekly trips to Europe from New York. The classmate observed that "professional women can successfully juggle only three balls at any one time." Women, and particularly women of color, are asked to juggle seven or eight balls (work, home, children, spouse/

partner, parents, friends, extended family assuming all are healthy, along with church/civic activities). It may sound brutal, but we do have to choose. Yet choosing which three balls to juggle can be stressful in and of itself.

Black Privilege—White Privilege

In the numerous non–profit organizations with which she is active, Jackie's goal has been to do more than just serve the various foreign policy, arts and alumni groups or benefit personally from their networking opportunities. In her non–profit arena, she has taken on the double burden which Bonita describes in the corporate world. Jackie has worked deliberately, consistently to make sure that she is not the only or the last woman (or man) of color in a center of power.

In almost all of these organizations, Jackie has embraced the role of a modern–day anthropologist, someone like Margaret Mead, studying the habits of the Park Avenue natives. When she has visited their homes, making her way past the gloved elevator operators, she has been shocked to learn how vicious their internecine battles can be.

In one notable instance, she had to laugh when one of the Park Avenue matrons said, "I perceive that you are a lady. Would you like to apply to become a member of my social club?" It was one of the exclusive, WASPy women's clubs featured in the show *Gossip Girl*. Sitting on the club's over-stuffed chintz sofas, sipping tea and nibbling on freshly baked macaroons were all welcome balms in jangly New York City. However, Jackie ultimately declined to apply for permanent membership in this bastion of privilege.

For Bonita, roaming the streets of San Francisco as a technology executive has also been an experience in anthropology. In the mass of hoodies (which, by the way, she doesn't think is her best look), she doesn't see that many people of color.

Rarely has either of us encountered or noticed overt racism, but we always are aware of our "only–ness."

Research about the stress of being "an only" describes the emotional tax that people/women of color face. But can we quantify it? Can we describe it clearly enough so that we and our allies can make genuine, lasting changes? One way could involve flipping the script and examining in detail so–called "white privilege."

There is a growing number of books and courses and strategies in the newly named "diversity industry." Among them, University of Washington professor and author Robin DiAngelo is selling workshops across the U.S. based on her book, *White Fragility: Why It's So Hard for White People to Talk About Racism*. The work builds on a 1988 paper by Wellesley University's Peggy McIntosh that unpacked the daily benefits of whiteness and, at the same time, the daily indignities of being of color.[53] Consider just a few of the items:

- No. 5: "I can go shopping alone most of the time, pretty well assured that I will not be followed or harassed."
- No. 10: "I can be pretty sure of having my voice heard in a group in which I am the only member of my race."
- No. 15: "I do not have to educate my children to be aware of systemic racism for their own daily physical protection."

- No. 20: "I can do well in a challenging situation without being called a credit to my race."
- No. 21: "I am never asked to speak for all the people of my racial group."
- No. 25: "If a traffic cop pulls me over or if the IRS audits my tax returns, I can be sure that I haven't been singled out because of my race."
- No. 41: "I can be sure that if I need legal or medical help, my race will not work against me."

Indignities like these are sometimes dubbed "microaggressions." What a clinical term. When you experience them, you can't quite believe it. Never does the encounter feel "micro."

Bonita—Shopping and Hotels

I rarely have time for a leisurely shopping trip, so when I enter a store, I am there to buy. I have always found shopping in luxury stores experiential, both for them and me. Sometimes I adorn myself with my best jewelry and clothing, but sometimes I dress down. Regardless, most days, I am ignored for fear that a commission will be foregone on a "browser." My tactic has been not to get mad, but to find a seat in the middle of the store and wait — and wait — until someone says, "Have you been helped?" I respond, "No, but I am here to buy x,y,z." My wait was so long in the Hermes store on Madison Avenue that I decided to let the CEO know that he was losing out on a lucrative market— Black women—so I wrote him a letter. I don't know if it was my letter, but I now find my in–store visits, which are rare, given my penchant for online shopping, much more pleasant.

The same happens when I travel. In hotels, I'm frequently given the worst room. I have a new tactic. Instead of waiting and calling from my less desirable room, I promptly wheel my luggage back to the receptionist and say, "Is this the best you have available for me?" It's amazing the other rooms that become available.

My favorite location is the Four Seasons Palo Alto where everybody knows your name, which makes me feel at home while I'm away from home. Most importantly, I feel gratitude for the Four Seasons as a company. My husband and I were married at the Four Seasons, Scottsdale, and the hospitality is amazingly non–judgmental worldwide.

After too many experiences of being "over–served" and followed while browsing, I have pretty much given up on shopping in Brick and Mortar stores. Jackie and I both prefer online shopping, where you never have to face an indignity.

Jackie—Restaurants and Elevators

I have started speaking out in restaurants. Routinely, I find I am shown a table near the kitchen or the bathrooms—even by hostesses of color. Now I always say loudly, "Why do you seat Black people at the worst tables?" I might get an eye roll from the hostess, but I am always moved to a better table. At one particular restaurant in a museum where I have been a major donor, I always make a reservation. There must be a note next to my name because now, I am always shown to MY preferred table. When I used to just drop in, I was always treated rudely. I complained to my friend who chairs the board of this institution and the rest, as they say, is history.

101

Elevators are also tricky. I was in one with a male friend, the then president of the Harvard Business School African–American Alumni Association. Though both of us were in business attire, a white woman shrunk back, as if in fear. When the doors opened on our floor, I looked at her and sneered, "Don't worry. We're not going to assault you." Recently, I was in an elevator at the famed Juilliard School, where I have taken music theory classes for several years. An old white man with a walker entered, looked up at me and asked if I was an opera singer. The confused look on my face must have registered because he began to apologize. I said, "No. I don't have the voice." Clearly, the old man's first thought was not I was just like him, an adult education student. If I wasn't a performer, why would I be there?

At a tribute to W. E. B. Du Bois at Carnegie Hall in 1968, Dr. Martin Luther King, Jr., explained how and why people of color have been subjected to an "emotional tax." His quote reminds us that nothing much has changed in America since people of color were first brought here 400 years ago. Dr. King said of Dr. Du Bois:

One idea he insistently taught was that Black people have been kept in oppression and deprivation by a poisonous fog of lies that depicted them as inferior, born deficient and deservedly doomed to servitude to the grave. Dr. Du Bois recognized that the keystone in the arch of oppression was the myth of inferiority, and he dedicated his brilliant talents to demolish it.[54]

So that's our task—demolishing the "myth of inferiority" of people of color—eliminating that "poisonous fog of lies." We can, and we must just—whoosh—blow it away. It's just fog. It's not true, even if it does seem real.

Yes, work is hard, and stress is inevitable, but it's not a requirement for leaders of color to be exemplars of exceptionalism every single day. Armor is heavy! As one leader has said: "Be yourself. Be authentic. Being who you think the 'firm' wants you to be, you're losing."

 **LIVING LOG**

We all know or have witnessed what NOT to do about stress. There are too many forms of toxic self–medication. But what's healthy and still works? We have listed a few questions and a few tips that we and friends employ.

- ❑ How often are you "the only" woman/person of color in a professional setting? In any setting?
- ❑ How do you feel about being an "only?"
- ❑ Do you feel you are treated differently when you are an "only?"
- ❑ How do you cope with being an "only?"
- ❑ Are you under stress at work? How do you manage that stress?
- ❑ Many people use exercise as a stress reliever: aerobics, weights, gyrotonics, running, yoga. What works for you?
    - ❑ Many people meditate each day. Before she gets out of bed each morning, one HBS alumna says she lays there quietly, visualizes what needs to be done that day and how to WIN.

❑ Do you have lifelong hobbies where being average is okay, something that just makes you happy, like Bonita's devotion to ballet? For Jackie, it's been needlepoint.

❑ How much do you sleep? Eight hours is supposed to be the most conducive for health and wellness.

❑ How healthy is your diet?

  ❑ Many experts are now recommending the Mediterranean diet — lots of seafood and fruit.

  ❑ Have you tried going vegetarian, even if it's only one day a week?

❑ Have you ever talked with a psychiatrist or therapist?

❑ Would you consider seeing a mental health professional? How would you select a therapist?

❑ How do you comfort yourself? What is your preferred method of self–care?

  ❑ One useful definition of self–care is whatever you can do to refill your tank, even if it means just going grocery shopping.

  ❑ There is a $10 Billion pampering industry. Even though a pedicure won't close the wage gap, it can make you happy. And happiness shouldn't be underrated.

❑ A young friend once said: "I have two choices; I can be great...or not great." Which are you?

❑ How many balls are you currently juggling? Which ones can you eliminate, for now?

❑ Do you know how to breathe and take deep breaths?

❑ Do you have a sacred space that brings you joy and comfort that's all yours?

❑ Do you praise others often?

❑ Do you express gratitude for someone or something every day?

❑ Do you simply check in with friends and co–workers? Just asking, "how are you doing?" can be a stress reducer for them and for you!

❑ Do you know how to "put on your oxygen mask first?"

❑ Do you have a life hack such as Headspace or the Calm app to calm your mind?

❑ Do you keep track of your weekly accomplishments?

    ❑ It can be inspirational to have this list in a place you see every day, like your bathroom mirror.

Bottom line: We are enough. While we may not be able to conquer the feelings or the stress of being lonely in our workplaces, we should not be alone as we ascend to leadership.

Don't forget: As the onlys, we also have a measure of Black privilege. We rise to the top, are isolated as the miracle leader and are then lavished with awards. We sometimes joke about the head "N" in charge. However, as we harness the credibility of our skills and hard work, we achieve more financial independence. We launch new companies. We gain power.

In a recent interview, a young Black woman said that one could think of being the only one as a blessing or a curse. She believes it is a blessing. She reminds us of the opening passage from M. Scott Peck, M.D.'s book, *The Road Less Traveled:*

"Life is difficult.

This is the great truth, one of the greatest truths. It is a great truth because once we truly see this truth, we transcend it. Once we truly know that life is difficult — once we truly understand and accept it — then life is no longer difficult. Because once it is accepted, the fact that life is difficult no longer matters."[55]

Chapter Four

Never Give Up!

T he advice "word clouds" generated by all 4,005 respondents of our *Women of Color in Business: Cross Generational Survey©* can be read in any number of ways. The simplest is to look at the words with the BOLDEST, largest print. These are the comments most often mentioned by our respondents.

All of the women across four generations and four races said: Never Give Up – Women in each generation and of each race said, "Never Give Up", when responding to the prompt, "What is the first piece of advice you'd give to a woman of color to achieve success in her career and in her work?"

- Asian women said: Work hard, Never give up, Don't let others define you.
  - Their areas of difference: Do your best, Be yourself.
  - It's also interesting that Asian women advised: Find your people but also Don't use your race and Stand up for yourself.

All Asian women

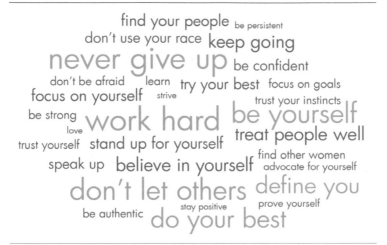

find your people be persistent
don't use your race keep going
never give up be confident
don't be afraid learn try your best focus on goals
focus on yourself strive
trust your instincts
be strong work hard be yourself
love
trust yourself stand up for yourself treat people well
find other women
speak up believe in yourself advocate for yourself
don't let others define you
be authentic stay positive prove yourself
do your best

Women of Color in Business: Cross Generational Survey©

- White women said: Never give up, Work hard, Don't let anyone stop you.
  - Unlike the other categories, white women advised: Don't focus on race.

All White women

do your best act
be tough get up just be yourself
have a good attitude
advocate for yourself ignore negative people fight
be strong
stay positive don't stop you can do anything achieve
never give up work towards your goals
find advocates know your worth work hard
knowledge believe in yourself stay true to yourself
don't let anyone stop you
be confident speak up get an education I don't know
don't focus on race
don't be afraid

Women of Color in Business: Cross Generational Survey©

- LatinX women said: Never give up, Work hard, Don't let anyone stop you.
  - They added: Keep pushing, Don't quit and Ignore negative people.
  - They also offered specific advice about race and gender: Don't let race or gender stop you, as well as Color does not define you.

All LatinX women

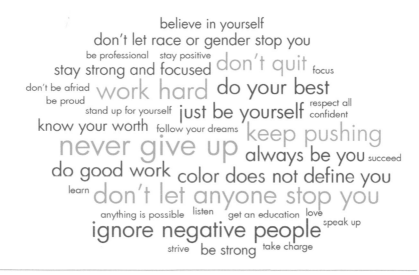

believe in yourself
don't let race or gender stop you
be professional   stay positive
stay strong and focused   don't quit   focus
don't be afriad   work hard   do your best
be proud
stand up for yourself   just be yourself   respect all
know your worth   follow your dreams   keep pushing
never give up   always be you   succeed
do good work   color does not define you
learn   don't let anyone stop you
anything is possible   listen   get an education   love
speak up
ignore negative people
strive   be strong   take charge

Women of Color in Business: Cross Generational Survey©

- Black women said: Never give up, Always be yourself, Work hard.
  - More than the other groups, Black women advised: Keep your head up, Don't let anyone stop you, Be Strong, Know your Worth as well as Get an education.
  - Black women were the only ones who said Put God first.

All Black women

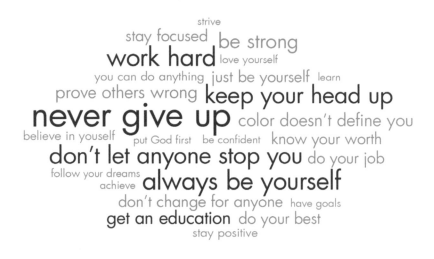

Women of Color in Business: Cross Generational Survey©

All of the advice is encouraging. All of it is worth following. It is significant that only the African American women stressed education. That finding is consistent with other surveys that show Black women are graduating from college and attending graduate schools in higher and higher numbers. The Insight Center for Community Economic Development in Oakland reports more and more Black women are pursuing college degrees. Twenty-six percent have earned a bachelor's degree or higher, up from 20% a decade ago.[56]

Ironically, our *Women of Color in Business: Cross Generational Survey©* found that we Black women are still subject to more scrutiny in hiring and more skepticism on the job. We tend to call the phenomenon being "over–credentialed and under–estimated."

Often, as HBS alumna Janelle Faulk noted, "We Black women respond to that extra scrutiny by keeping our heads down, by staying in a comfortable role, excelling in place." Janelle's advice: "Take risks! Break out of the comfortable role!"

And yet taking risks, filling leadership roles with passion and creativity can sometimes generate isolation, the fear of making a mistake as well as backlash in your own office and/or among your clients. But is just keeping your head down an acceptable alternative? Many of our parents taught us to do just that, to follow their example by being cautious and merely hardworking and that's how we'll get promoted. Times have changed, though.

Taking risks can generate tremendous rewards, often catapulting your career, if done well. How? Align with a senior leader or two, enhance your skills with outside courses or mentors, become indispensable to a client, understand the differences between a mistake and a failure, or even possibly by seeking a new opportunity in a new environment.

Kimberly Foster—Being Underestimated

Kimberly Foster joined a large consulting firm right out of undergraduate school. She was the only Black person in the company's valuations department. After four years, she headed to Harvard Business School, but before she departed, she had a track record of success. She devoted 110% to her job, received great performance reviews and often led teams as they interfaced with clients.

As a young, Black woman, she found that too often, she experienced what she called "microaggressions." She was shocked and angered the first time she spoke up in a meeting and the client, a white male, turned to another white male on Kimberly's team, a man more junior than Kimberly, to get assurance that what she had said was accurate. He was double–checking her point! "It irked me. Just because the white male looked like the client, he was assumed to be more qualified. It didn't matter that I was the more senior person in the room."

Kimberly recalled that she stayed calm and continued to lead the meeting as planned. What she did after the meeting, though, reflected her maturity and the can–do/must–do spirit of many women of color. She outworked the white men.

"At our firm, it was customary for the most junior person on the team to send email follow–ups or just own email communications with the client in general. It's viewed as a non–revenue gener-ating administrative task. However, given that the client sought validation from the white man in the room, I decided to take on those tasks so the client viewed me as his main contact and advisor. Unfortunately, it was a lot more work than I needed to do and caused me to stay later than most people on my team on most days. However, the client's attitude towards me shifted, and he saw me as his trusted advisor." Kimberly continued: "Unfortunately, this wasn't the first time that this happened – and it has happened with a lot of other people. It's actually expected now–so I make sure to take up a lot of space in meetings. I do this by making my presence known very quickly, sitting at the big table even if it's a meeting with more senior people and chiming in whenever I have some-thing to say."

The prevalence of these "microaggressions" helped convince Kimberly to apply to graduate school. In 2018, she was selected as one of just the 11% of applicants admitted from the 9,886 who applied. Kimberly carved her own winning path. Don't get mad. Get into Harvard!

The Evolution of "Failure"

In our current business environment, failure is no longer seen as a death knell, as the end of the professional road. Especially in the Wild West, go–go atmosphere of Silicon Valley, failure is seen as a necessary step on the road to ultimate success. A 30–year–old African American male entrepreneur told us: "Failure is good unless you get knocked out of the game. Hopefully, you can learn enough to rocket out the next time. Failure is understanding your limitations and how far you can grow. You can learn more from a terrible meeting—so stay the course. If a meeting is a disaster, you can tell your therapist afterwards that you barfed when you got out of the room."

A number of successful businesspeople will concede privately that failure made them better. They will tell you it was a useful exercise and that it was especially informative to see how they reacted to failure. Many saw their powering through failures as components of the "grit" and perseverance for which women of color are famous.

And then there's the historical perspective. One successful, serial entrepreneur remembered what his mother often told him as a child. His mother, the granddaughter of a runaway slave, reminded him he wasn't in chains, wasn't being chased by dogs and didn't have to live by his wits in a swamp. So, stop complaining!

Alrighty then.

HBS alumna Beverly Anderson believes adversity only makes success that much sweeter. Here is her description of a workplace experience she considers one of the most tumultuous, yet path–altering in her career:

Beverly Anderson—Couples Counseling

One of the most developmental times in my career was during a phase at a financial services company where my leader and I just didn't get each other. Our relationship was so strained at one point that we were sent to "couples counseling." That's what I call joint executive coaching.

During this period in my career, I dreaded going to work in the mornings, and I would curl up in a ball on Sunday nights because I knew every interaction would be contentious, devaluing and demotivating. Nothing that I said or did–from his perspective–was ever going to be good enough. I was miserable. I truly thought about quitting. However, I knew I was more than capable of leading my team, developing sound business strategies and delivering results. I even tried to change my physical appearance to be "more acceptable"–to fit in. For a successful overachiever, this experience was debilitating.

One day, recalling the words of Rosa Parks, I drew upon the inner faith and strength that I knew I had. Ms. Parks had said: "I have learned over the years that when one's mind is made up, this diminishes fear; knowing what must be done, does away with fear." I knew I had to be me, play my game my way and let the chips fall where they may.

As I began to exude my new found confidence and resolve, I was soon discovered and rescued by a woman who would go on to be my most influential leader and mentor. She saw something in me that this other guy never would—my capacity to lead and win. While I may have failed in that role, the lessons I learned about leaning on my strength, my perseverance and my faith sustain me to this day.

New research is showing that failure, particularly if it comes early in one's career, can result in a stronger career in the long term. Kellogg School of Management at Northwestern researchers have published new data in the journal, *Nature Communications*. They found that 10 years out, young, statistically identical scientists have stronger careers if they had suffered early setbacks.

Melanie Stefan, a lecturer at Edinburgh Medical School, endorses the practice of keeping a log of failures as a source of motivation, a way to assess the lessons you've learned. She said: "Sometimes I look back on my rejections and see how much I've actually struggled to be where I am. That's a powerful reminder that I deserve to be here." It is also, she said, "a good reminder of how much you've tried."[57]

Does/can this strategy work as well, if you're Black? What would Bonita do?

- Address your mistake head–on and admit what you **learned**. Here's a secret: Those who try new projects or never–been–done–before strategies grow faster as leaders.
- Don't get mad. Use your emotions as your Trojan horse to get ahead. Sometimes, our ideas are just too early.
- Seek counsel from others; understand perception versus reality.
- Know when to hold, fold or walk away.

- Don't make it personal.
- Be willing to share your mistake secrets.
- Give yourself only 24 hours for a pity party then move on. A warm bath works wonders.
- Fail with grace.
- Embrace the zigzag career philosophy. You might find a better fit in another department, on another team or even with another employer. Sometimes you can move forward by moving laterally.

Whoa—Rewind—Why Are We Focusing on "Failure" Rather than "Mistakes?"

We had almost finished writing this section when we went, Whoa! All of this focus on failure struck us as somewhat useful but potentially counter productive. Jackie had been extremely dismayed by the seeming embrace of the notion of failure when she attended a career training session for young leaders of color in the media. The young leaders defended the notion of failure as a component of innovation. Okay. But Jackie preferred to look at performance from a more positive, glass–half–full perspective, especially now, in an era of fake news. How might we reconcile the two concepts?

We decided to go to the dictionary and examine the definitions and synonyms of "failure" and "mistake." And then, we examined some relevant principles developed by Ray Dalio, the famed hedge fund leader and philanthropist.

A failure, the dictionary says, is a lack of success. Synonyms include defeat, collapse, debacle, disaster, screwup.

A mistake, however, is defined as an act of judgment that is misguided or wrong. Synonyms include omission, slip, blunder, miscalculation.

Ah–ha. Sure, we've all made mistakes and most of us have vowed never to make the same one again. That's learning. That's the basis of wisdom. But abject failure, disaster, screwup?

Successful cosmetics entrepreneur and HBS alumna, Amanda E. Johnson, differentiates between the two concepts. She states that the differences reflect both race/gender and size of organization parameters.

Amanda E. Johnson's Perspective

Amanda E. Johnson's perspective A mistake can happen and the machine/the organization can keep going. A failure is when the machine stops. The difference is related to the relative impact.

In my experience, a privileged white man can have a failure in the tech world and he can come back from that failure, even if it's the result of sheer stupidity.

But people of color can NOT have an abject failure. If you don't have wealth, the right people backing you and a track record of previous successes, you're going to have to package your failure effectively to move on—and even then, with difficulty. If I were to fail in my startup, the narrative would be that Black women didn't know what to do with that kind of money. If I were to fail, investors would make my failure one of all Black women and would justify the conclusion that white men must be better bets for investment.

Ray Dalio's *Principles for Success* offers a different perspective. He fears mediocrity and boredom more than failure. He says that "pain + reflection = progress, especially when you're after ambitious goals." He urges business people to know which mistakes are acceptable and unacceptable. Also, he urges leaders to create a culture in which making mistakes is okay, but what's not okay is not learning from them.[58]

This "mistakes–based–learning" philosophy is a kinder way of approaching work, even in the technology and entrepreneurial ecosystems.

Bonita—I Rise, I Rise, I Rise

The big "F" word always brings a few knots to my stomach. You analyze, work hard, and sometimes things just don't pan out. This has happened to me, as it will to most people who are fervently seeking the edge of possibility.

Going for the edge means you are seeking innovative approaches and are willing to stumble. I learned early on, during my automotive journey, that innovation works best when you disrupt yourself.

Ballet provides an excellent metaphor. The best way to learn a double or triple pirouette is to try, fall, lose your balance and adjust your alignment. But when you do nail it, the feeling is pure exhilaration. In the end, it's always worth trying.

Within the tech industry, you are in a sandbox for innovation where psychological safety, empowerment and explosive growth resemble a hockey stick rule. As Ray Dalio says in his Principles: Life and Work, *know how to "fail well" and recognize that "mistakes are a natural part of the evolutionary process." He reinforces the notion of "mistakes–based learning," which I have embraced throughout my career along with being self–reflective around "which patterns of mistakes" were "products of weakness."*

In 1994, while I was leading Consumer Strategy for the Chrysler Group, I commissioned a Buyer Satisfaction study through a consulting firm to examine trends for the future state of automotive car buying. As a non–automotive executive coming from IBM versus the traditional automotive career on–ramps, I knew firsthand the angst associated with the buying process. Our groundbreaking work elevated the awareness of the trend that power was shifting from the dealer and factory to the consumer and that technology would continue to affect the buying process at all consumer touch points.

We pulled together a small, rather rogue team of believers across Chrysler, our agency and technology partners. I was the only woman and, if I'm honest, we were a confident (perhaps even arrogant) crew. After declaring "the dealer franchise under siege," we proceeded to design and implement the "New World Project" called Modus, which launched with the slogan: "It's about time... your time." The slogan was a nod to our supporting research that the buying process was both inefficient and lengthy.

It was a tumultuous process as we rattled the C–suite and our dealers with the advent of a new way of doing business. We launched this new process in a Jeep dealership with some apprehension. While we were asked to initiate this proof of concept with a car dealership, as tech–savvy outsiders, we knew online technology would cause the greater seismic shift. I was the anointed leader of a bold and mission–driven team. As the project stalled for numerous reasons, someone asked me a poignant question that I use to this day: "Do you want to be right, or do you want to be effective?" While I was right that digital technology would empower consumers, needless to say, it was not my finest hour. In hindsight, there were things I could have finessed better.

I staunchly defend the road toward innovation to this day and support fearless experimentation. When my project was terminated, I did "fail well." Every partner relationship and financial details were closed out with perfection, humility and honor. Given my penchant for embracing industry upheaval, I believe no automotive executive or dealer who crossed my path during this period was surprised when I joined Google to build and lead the entire automotive industry through its first phase of digital transformation.

I am forever grateful to Chrysler for embracing early experimentation, staying true to their DNA of innovation and absorbing the tension of change. It was the company's track record for innovation (e.g., Minivan, PT Cruiser, Viper, etc.) and surviving multiple near–death business failures that drove me to accept their employment offer in the first place. Of all the automotive companies, they had the marks of an entrepreneur.

I had previously had a base of experience in fearless entrepreneurial experimentation from my founding and launching of a venture without any experience. In a start–up, you are doing it all: payroll, business plans, raising capital and marketing! My first entrepreneurial venture, which my partner and I called One Moment in Time, was conceived in 1989 as a formal wear rental concept (without the internet) and was recognized by Entrepreneur *magazine as one of the "hottest businesses" in 1993. Fast forward 20 years, in 2009, Rent the Runway, essentially my original concept, launched as a direct to consumer platform business and is currently valued at $1Billion.*

Witness the eye–opening TED Talk by Bill Gross, founder of the first U.S.–based startup accelerator Idealab, where he showcases his research on the common threads that explain why a start–up would succeed or fail. He found the biggest predictor of success was "timing." If we take an honest approach with ourselves and think of ourselves as start–ups, we are likely to identify when we are "ahead of our time or timed perfectly."

Factors Impacting Success

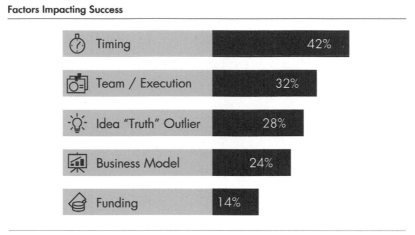

Timing	42%
Team / Execution	32%
Idea "Truth" Outlier	28%
Business Model	24%
Funding	14%

Bill Gross, TED Conference, June 2015

Similar to skiing, you must learn how to fall in business, and it is best if we learn how to fail forward.

With both of these ventures, one corporate and one entrepreneurial, I found out that sometimes it's not you, it's timing. Many lessons were learned. However, I learned two major things about myself: my comfort with disruption and my desire to further hone my leadership skills to shepherd others more successfully through ambiguous processes.

The Black Imposter Syndrome—Tokenism and Divine Diversions

"What happens to Black women is that we become a caricature–people will literally take our voices, they will take the things from us that they like...our style, our swag..but then we're demonized, we are angry, we are too loud, too everything."[59]

121

That was former First Lady Michelle Obama's unhappy analysis of today's woman of color "brand." She made the comment during her book tour appearance in London in December 2018, when the Duchess of Sussex Meghan Markle was in the audience.

We can understand why both women might agree with this assessment. Both have been lionized, but they have also been targeted by internet trolls, racists and media outlets ready to defame outstanding women of color. Defiling our images and invoking standards of so–called "acceptable beauty," they try to undermine and minimize our superb progress and stellar accomplishments.

Growing up in the 1950s and 60s, we did not have a Michelle Obama or a Meghan Markle to inspire us. Our families, our role models did that for us. We relied on the advice and the strong psychological armor provided by our fathers and grandparents. But every now and then, the barrage of external assaults slipped in and had an impact.

Bonita wanted to go into broadcast journalism, but when a career conference exhibitor said her eyes were too small, she abandoned that dream and pursued a business career instead. Jackie might have been a candidate for a paying corporate board after leaving CBS News, but she didn't challenge headhunters who said her communications skills were less valuable than finance or high–tech expertise. Instead, she chose to strengthen her administrative and managerial skills by taking on senior volunteer roles in a variety of non–profit organizations and joining several non–profit boards.

As we chatted with other HBS alumnae, we uncovered other "routes not taken" or what we call "divine diversions."

Amanda E. Johnson wanted to study politics. In high school, her dream had been to grow up to become a United States senator and change the world. But the director of the honors program at Howard University pulled her aside before freshman classes even began. Impressed by Amanda's math scores on her college admissions tests, the advisor urged Amanda to become a finance major. The new focus led her to Wall Street and Harvard Business School and now, to a successful entrepreneurial career. She might yet choose to pursue a political career at some point, but in the meantime, she's built a strong business foundation along with genuine wealth for herself and her community. "Now," Amanda says, "I see how I can have more impact in life overall."

When Denise Murrell was a high school student in Gastonia, North Carolina, she wanted to be a history professor. Instead, she studied economics, earned her MBA from Harvard and had a long career at financial firms like Citigroup and Institutional Investor. She told *The New York Times* that her mother reminded Denise of her abandoned ambition decades later, when she began her career transition, eventually earning a Ph.D. in art history at Columbia University. Denise's scholarship produced an extraordinary book and groundbreaking exhibit, *Posing Modernity: The Black Model from Manet to Matisse to Today* at Columbia's Wallach Art Gallery. Some half a million visitors saw her work in Paris at the Musee D'Orsay in the summer of 2019. She was subsequently named an associate curator at the Metropolitan Museum of Art in New York City, only the third African American curator ever at the world–renowned museum. What was her innovation? Denise saw, really saw, Black figures in scores of famous paintings and sculptures, figures deliberately ignored for centuries by the "canon," the traditional, mostly white art history industry. She went further and contextualized these Black figures. When they were not invented, she determined who the real people were, the actual models, and how and where they lived and worked amid the artists who painted and sculpted them. Her exhibitions and scholarship have revealed an overlooked Black presence within the artistic circles central to the foundation of modern art.[60]

Did any of us succumb to even a scintilla of the dreaded "imposter syndrome" that plagues so many women–so many people–of color? Did we ever buy into that old saying: "Growth doesn't happen in comfortable places?" Frankly, for us, no! Our respective families gave us the confidence to march boldly–albeit alone–into any and every room that we may have wanted to enter. But our attitudes and experiences are not the norm.

Author Lincoln Hill summarized the origins and symptoms of the imposter syndrome:

"In addition to combating racial stereotypes, questioning their intellectual abilities and sense of belonging, Black women must also contend with specific gendered racial messaging and stereotypes such as the 'strong Black woman,' 'the angry Black woman,' 'the hypersexual Black woman,' and 'the invisible and silenced Black woman.'

Consequently, a Black woman suffering from impostor syndrome will likely have distinctive reasoning for why she feels like an impostor when compared to a white woman. For Black women, the impostor syndrome might be triggered by feeling othered in predominantly white or exclusive spaces, navigating gendered racial microaggressions on the job or in class, stereotype threat, or merely existing in a culture that

124

either ignores or objectifies them. So, the way we understand and discuss the impostor syndrome has to account for these different social realities."[61]

Objectively, neither of us would say we suffered too much or that we didn't actually earn our successes. Amanda and Denise would surely agree. We all had the necessary brainpower and confidence to compete and compete successfully. We all have spent so much time being "othered" that we took it as a normal state.

"A hint of the imposter syndrome may have kicked in for me during my business ascension," Bonita said. "Whenever I was selected for an honor or promotion, I kept asking myself, was I selected as the token or the real candidate? In fact, it didn't matter because in all cases, I was underestimated, aptly prepared and mentally sturdy to be a pioneer. Throughout my career, I have broken barriers and boundaries as the highest-ranking or first African American woman to hold the position. Someone must be first and I always felt confident to challenge why not me."

The *Oxford Dictionary* defines a "token" as "a member of a minority group included in an otherwise homogeneous set of people in order to give the appearance of diversity." By now, much published research has convinced (or should have convinced) most companies that recruiting adequate representation is healthy for the bottom line. On the other hand, when HBS Professor Rosabeth Moss Kanter published her groundbreaking research on tokenism for women in 1977, she highlighted a more troubling aspect. She stated that "proportional representation suggests that tokens should experience more work stress and psychological symptoms than non-tokens."

While she did not research women of color in her study, the mental burden of being a "Black only" is now widely recognized and was reflected in our *Women of Color in Business: Cross Generational Survey©*. Our research found that young women of all colors, particularly the Gen Z women ages 16–22, are no longer prepared to suffer in silence. As this new generation enters the workforce, they expect a helping hand from their supervisors. We call the phenomenon GD–generational diversity.

Our research puts all leaders and managers on notice: Your guidance for women now matters for their progress within your organization as well as for your ability to retain them in your workforce.

How helpful do you believe the guidance you receive from managers or supervisors will be in your work progress?

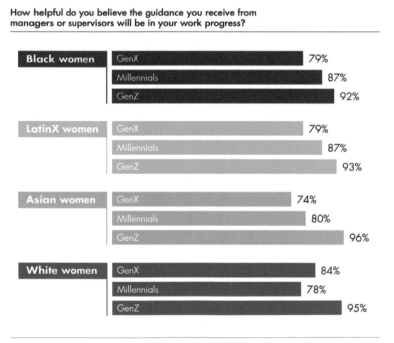

Black women		
GenX	79%
Millennials	87%
GenZ	92%

LatinX women		
GenX	79%
Millennials	87%
GenZ	93%

Asian women		
GenX	74%
Millennials	80%
GenZ	96%

White women		
GenX	84%
Millennials	78%
GenZ	95%

Women of Color in Business: Cross Generational Survey©

Bonita's and Jackie's Lament

Why haven't hundreds of thousands of women of color followed in our footsteps in the last several decades? Why haven't the achievements of the few generated substantive, widespread progress for the many? And did our individual successes make it possible for "the man" to pat himself on the back, metaphorically, and thereby alleviate the need to welcome more of us into the inner sanctums of power?

Clearly, these are all rhetorical questions for which there are no real answers. We were heartened, though, when we read an interview with Ellen Ochoa, the first Latina in space. When asked about the imposter syndrome and specific advice for Latinas in STEM fields, she offered sage advice, "While there may be extra attention on you, the actual job/career is no different. Focus on understanding what success looks like, working hard, delivering results, and being the best team member that you can be."[62]

Amen, Sister!

Hell Hath No Fury—Like An Educated Black Woman Scorned

Tokenism—failures—microaggressions! Yes, there are genuine reasons for our anger! Assaults on the inner confidence and the very self–images of women of color today seem to be on the rise. In fact, some social scientists have crafted a racial and gendered hierarchy of anger. Jackie heard these descriptions at a Harvard Business School conference on Gender and Work in the spring of 2019. This is how it goes:

- White male anger is perceived as a civic virtue.
- Black male anger is perceived as criminality.
- Black female anger makes people uncomfortable.
  - They get angry back, and it's perceived that they are difficult, no matter how justified the anger is.
- Power accrues to men when they display anger, but it penalizes women.
- The paternalistic and infantilizing stereotypes are the angry Black woman, the crazy white woman, the hot Latina and the sad Asian girl.

As activist Soraya Chemaly, author of *"Rage Becomes Her,"* said, "Anger and self-care can produce political action. Self-care is a politically revolutionary act." And leaders of "the Squad," Congresswomen Alexandria Ocasio Cortez and Ayanna Pressley, have put it bluntly: "The landscape is changing. Millennial women are embracing and activating their anger."

Yes, we're angry and here are just two specific examples of why:

- Across the country, Black women are having to defend, and even legislate, the way they wear their hair in schools and in some workplaces. In December 2019, Senator Cory Booker (D–N.J.) and Rep. Cedric L. Richmond (D–La.) introduced bills in both the U.S. Senate and House of Representatives that echo laws passed in a number of states. The measures would specifically prohibit discrimination against styles such as braids, twists or locs. "Discrimination against black hair is discrimination against Black people," Booker said in a statement. "Implicit and explicit biases against natural hair are deeply ingrained in workplace norms and society at large."[63]

- Black women are beginning to create emotionally and physically safe workspaces that specifically address their needs, spaces in which they need never face threats or even just questions about their right to exist. They used to be called our kitchens or beauty parlors, even the "Black table" at the college cafeteria. Now, they are being constructed in cities around the U.S.[64]

Opening the Glass Door

We want to create a new metaphor to replace the old ones that limit women in the workplace. The "glass ceiling" has been around for decades. Jackie once heard a slightly shocking definition of the term at a conference at Barnard College. "The ceiling isn't made of glass. If it were merely glass, women would have smashed through it long ago. The ceiling isn't glass. It's a thick layer of white men!"

More recently, the "glass cliff" concept was developed by Dr. Michelle Ryan and Professor Alex Haslam from the School of Psychology at the University of Exeter. As described in their research, "the glass cliff examines what happens when women and members of minority groups are appointed to leadership positions that are associated with an increased risk of criticism and failure during times of crisis or downturn. These glass cliffs are thus seen as more precarious than those of white men, and they tend to occur in fields as diverse as finance, politics, technology and academia."

129

Let's reject both of those metaphors and replace them with a new one: A Glass Door! When Bonita first moved to the New York area from Denver, she was mesmerized by the doormen. They were everywhere—at apartments, hotels, stores, and they were all men. They would greet you with grace and a warm welcome.

As we begin a new decade, shouldn't we declare the "ceiling" and the "cliff" antiquated? Who wants to climb and break a ceiling or fall off a cliff? Both activities seem exhausting and physically harmful!

We should have our "doormen," the businessmen in 2020 plus, our allies both Black and white, adopt the attitude of welcoming and grace. They could simply open the door for us and welcome us into their world, their world of venture funding, C–suites, boardrooms, places of genuine power. We promise we'll come prepared to deliver 110% just as we always have in the past.

Always A Next Chapter—Defining Your Destiny

We began this chapter with the advice that our 4,005 knowledge workers provided in our proprietary survey: Never Give Up! Work Hard! Be Yourself! Don't Let Anyone Stop You!

We have followed that advice, and this book is one result.

By teaming up with each other, with our Harvard Business School alumnae and now with you, we are creating a next chapter, a new destiny, a glass door to the blessings that accompany a group of Black unicorns all pulling in the same direction, all pulling on behalf of one another, recognizing our collective power.

We are piercing the fog of inferiority that oppressors–past, present and future–would impose upon us to limit our options. We are blowing that fog away.

We can't wait to see what comes next!

 **LIVING LOG**

❑ Under what circumstances do you feel you have failed? How did you react?

❑ Can you identify the difference between a mistake and a failure? How should your reaction change?

❑ Have you ever struggled with the "imposter syndrome?" How did you overcome those feelings?

❑ How often do you observe other women of color struggling? How do you react?

❑ What kinds of words/actions would you welcome from someone who observed YOU struggling?

❑ Do you experience "microaggressions" as an "only" — an only person of color or only woman–in business settings? How do you react? How should you react?

❑ Is it ever appropriate to express your anger? When and how?

❑ How do you maneuver zigs and zags, ups and downs in your career?

❑ What was your childhood career ambition? Might it still be in your future? How?

Chapter Five

Dreaming of Allies

arlem Renaissance poet Langston Hughes wrote so eloquently, "Hold fast to dreams." Succeeding inside corporations has never been easy. And yet, women of color traditionally hold fast to dreams. Without the dream of a genuine meritocracy, without the dream that our ambitions can be recognized and fulfilled, life can be "a barren field."

Too few of us have succeeded to date. Although women of color are 18% of the U.S. population, we represented only 4% of C–Level positions in 2018, falling far below white men (68%) and white women (19%), according to a LeanIn.org and McKinsey study.[65]

Even graduating from a prestigious business or law school doesn't help much. Studies conducted during 2018's 50th anniversary of the African American Student Union at Harvard Business School found that of the 532 African American women who earned their MBAs at HBS between 1977 and 2015, including Bonita and Jackie, only 67 (13%) have achieved the highest–ranking executive positions. Our numbers pale in comparison to 161 (19%) of

African American men and 40% of a matched sample of 150 non–African American HBS alumni.[66]

Reality can be "a barren field." But as tennis' GOAT (greatest of all time) Serena Williams reminded us: "... being strong is never easy. Not in this world we are living in. Standing up for yourself is not going to be easy, but it's always eventually respected." In an interview in *Allure magazine*, Williams said, "Those are the people who've made a difference in this world, people who stand up for what's right. If you look at history, those are the people who you really remember. And at the time, oh, my God, it seemed impossible."[67] For those of us who have succeeded to date, our paths have frequently been smoothed by white men, the only allies possible. In this chapter, we want to thank them. We also want to further help them help us. For future female leaders of color, we want to offer possible insights and tips to help you utilize this vast and critically important asset.

Research cited by scholars Laura Morgan Roberts, Anthony J. Mayo and David A. Thomas "has indicated that CEOs (and lower–level managers) who champion diversity are penalized, unless they are white males."[68]

We know our potential white male allies are watching us, but what they may not know is that we are watching them. They probably don't know how many of us get through the difficult days by, as criminal justice lawyer Bryan Stevenson writes, sustaining "hope through a grace–filled pursuit of justice and mercy."

Yet, when Black women executives are feeling a little less "grace–filled," a frequent complaint sounds like this: "It's not enough that we have to run faster and be smarter. They have to LIKE us too!"

Professor Joan C. Williams, director of the Center for WorkLife Law at the University of California Hastings College of the Law, has interviewed some 200 success-ful women about the "likeability trap" and has conclud-ed: "Women who behave in authoritative ways risk being disliked as insufferable prima donnas, pedantic school-marms or witchy women." She could have added as an "angry Black woman."[69]

Women, and women of color in particular, have never experienced what appears to be the easy acceptance accorded to white men in the workplace. Only recently has the phrase "white privilege" been cited as the rationale. Professors Roberts, Mayo and Thomas quote a useful, albeit harsh defi-nition of "white privilege" from a 2017 study: "White privi-lege is an absence of the consequences of racism. An absence of structural discrimination, an absence of your race being viewed as a problem first and foremost."[70]

If we are unable to eliminate structural discrimination or the "problem" of our race, how are we women of color to survive and thrive?

Early in her career, Jackie observed that many of the "white guys" don't internalize completely the "privilege" that we attribute to them. Many of them carry around insecurities that women and people of color could never imagine, inner doubts about their backgrounds or capabilities. Race or gender may not be their Achilles' heel, but if you scratch the surface, you'll find that everyone carries around insecurities.

Here are two examples:

- A politician in Boston, with Irish Catholic roots, became a good friend. He told me how insecure he and his brothers felt around Harvard alums of his generation. He was a graduate of an excellent local college and its law school but those degrees weren't enough to make him feel equal to the Harvard guys. He conceded that he and his brothers were able to "pass," because their aunt worked at a poshy men's store and therefore, they had the proper wardrobe. But at his core, he never felt equal, comfortable or completely secure in the Harvard circles. Just being "white and male" could never be enough in the one and only place it mattered, his psyche.
- Long–time Harvard Business School Dean John McArthur passed away in the summer of 2019. In his tribute to McArthur, Walter Ross, a co–founder of the HBS African–American Alumni Association, recalled how supportive and creative the Dean had been when the group was trying to launch.

  Ross attributed that support to the fact that McArthur held on to a certain humility and perhaps a bit of insecurity as a result of being Canadian with a forestry undergraduate degree. Ross wrote: "It's not lost on me that Dean McArthur came to HBS in the 1950s from Canada's westernmost province where he had earned a bachelor's degree in forestry and where according to Dean McArthur, his boss at the lumber company he worked for suggested that he pursue an MBA at Harvard. He came to the business school, then, as most of us black students did a generation later, as an outsider."

Knowing that many white guys have genuine insecurities conveyed to Jackie a certain sense of power as well as compassion. It may be a cliché but "hurt people hurt others."

Early in her leadership journey, Bonita received an unexpected confidence boost from one of her Harvard Business School professors. After she had led a team of classmates in a Business Policy Field Study project, Professor C. Roland Christensen sent her an "atta–girl" note. She kept it and re–reads the note whenever a seed of doubt about her capabilities starts to sprout. He wrote: *"Bonita: You have great leadership potential! Don't ever settle for anything else! Your career will be sharing and successful. CRC"*

This hasn't been the first time Bonita's career and confidence have been supported by white male superiors. She can point to situations in which the white guys have been far more helpful than female superiors. She has never had a Black female superior. (As an aside, Jackie has never had a Black female direct superior either.)

As a woman with ambition, I must admit that early in my career, I found most executive women weren't as helpful compared to the growing camaraderie I am witnessing and sharing firsthand today. It's early in your career when you need those "career whisperers" who are willing to offer the "radical candor" that is especially actionable. I had one woman manager whom I applauded, during this instance, for her ability to step outside of the woman executive meme. One day at IBM, I just couldn't take it anymore. We all wore these suits with stiff white or plain–colored shirts and pussy bows. The day I decided to buck the trend and wear a dress, my branch manager declared it was a longing of hers as well. She wore a dress the next day! It was a triumphant feeling knowing I could create a new trend. Based on my personal experience, I vowed to "carry a ladder everywhere." I have subsequently owned my femininity at work and consistently tried to help younger women and younger employees of color. This usually involved working behind the scenes, advocating for talent and NOT being that woman destined for hell.

Even on the battlefield that is work, the vast majority of senior female executives of color can point to a white male boss who believed in her and helped propel her career. They are the ones with the power, after all, and sometimes, often, they have been forces for good. "You can absolutely be what you can't see! That's what innovators and disruptors do," says Kimberly Bryant, founder of Black Girls Code. "Even as pioneers, allies are the necessary seed funding to accelerate our ascension."[71]

White men can and have played a variety of roles: allies, mentors and/or sponsors. There are important differences between the three terms. An ally is in a superior position and can help explain the culture of an organization and provide tips for succeeding. A sponsor is in the rooms where decisions about pay and promotions are made and can advocate for a more junior person. A mentor can be anyone, in or out of a specific organization, who can be a truth–teller, a reality check, a cheerleader, a shoulder to cry on and a role model.

Whatever the definitions, the recent McKinsey & Company study, Women in the Workplace *2018* (four years of data, 279 companies), found results that are more commonplace perhaps, than the experiences we have had:

- Women don't get sponsored, supported or mentored as often as their male counterparts. This shows up in navigating politics, to plum assignments, to favor expressed in talent reviews or access to senior leaders.

- Only 27% of male managers have never had an interaction with senior leaders about their work, while 32% of white women and 41% of women of color never have.

So that's the larger problem: by and large, they don't know us; they don't interact with us; and so, they can't promote us. And the costs — the actual costs — of the disconnect are real.

Bloomberg has cited 2019 research by the salary website, PayScale, which found something new. The headline said it all: "The White–Male Mentorship Premium: New research shows some corporate sponsors are more successful at advancing their protégés — and that's hurting women of color."

According to the study: "More than 98,000 people were asked to disclose their salaries and details about their workplace advocate, if they had one. Around two–thirds of those polled provided data on the race or gender of their sponsor, in addition to their pay." More than half reported having a sponsor at work, but:

- Of the white m ale respondents who said they have a sponsor, 90% said their sponsor was white.
- Among Black and Hispanic women who said they have a sponsor, 60% said their sponsor was white.
- A study released earlier this year said most executives choose protégés who look like them.
- The survey found that Black women who have a Black sponsor reported making 11.3% less than Black women with a white sponsor.

- Hispanic women with a Hispanic sponsor make 15.5% less than Hispanic women with a white sponsor.
- Black and Hispanic women who have no sponsor at all are paid 5% less than those who do.[72]

Our *Women of Color in Business: Cross Generational Survey©* of 4,005 American desk or knowledge workers confirmed many aspects of the other surveys. Black, LatinX and especially Asian women said they seek support at work from people of races other than their own. Only white women said they seek allies from within their same race.

Likewise, Black, LatinX and Asian women said women at work can be allies and advocates. Interestingly, though, white women had the strongest reaction when asked about the gender of allies and advocates. Only 37% (the smallest percentage of the four races) said white men have been their most important allies and advocates.

Would you say your most important allies or advocates at work have been:

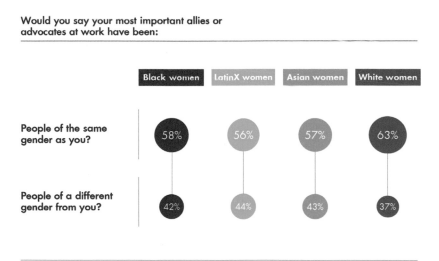

Women of Color in Business: Cross Generational Survey©

139

Would you say your most important allies or
advocates at work have been:

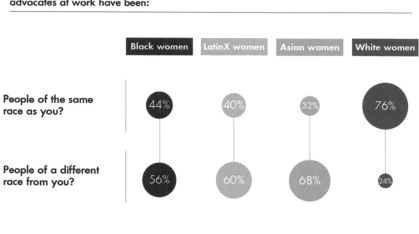

Women of Color in Business: Cross Generational Survey©

Strategies for White Male Leaders

So, are we doomed? A few studies are providing clues, specific strategies for white male leaders to use to bridge cultural, demographic and attitudinal gulfs.

Deloitte Australia studied inclusive leaders from Australia, New Zealand, Singapore, Hong Kong, Canada and the U.S. and found that the successful ones "possess six fundamental traits that foster diversity on their teams." The full descriptions are found in the actual study, but here is the essence of the six traits. We have underlined two that are among Bonita's father's Four Cs:

Commitment. In addition to a belief in the business case, inclusive leaders are driven by their values, including a deep–seated sense of fairness that, for some, is rooted in personal experience.

Courage. Inclusive leaders aren't afraid to challenge entrenched organizational attitudes and practices that yield homogeneity. They are not afraid to display humility by acknowledging their personal limitations and seeking contributions from others to overcome them.

Cognizance of bias. Inclusive leaders seek to implement policies, processes and structures to prevent organizational biases from stifling diversity and inclusion.

Curiosity. In addition to accessing a more diverse array of viewpoints, inclusive leaders' ability to engage in respectful questioning, actively listen to others and synthesize a range of ideas that make the people around them feel valued, respected and represented.

Cultural intelligence. Culturally intelligent leaders who are typically extroverted and demonstrative will make an effort to show restraint when doing business with individuals whose cultures value modesty or humility.

Collaborative. Inclusive leaders create an environment in which all individuals feel empowered to express their opinions freely with the group. They also realize that diversity of thinking is critical to effective collaboration.[73]

The bottom line seems to be that leaders should display "humility" in dealing with diverse teams.

So how did we and any of our peers survive and thrive? We were tough, mentally and physically, perhaps a precondition of being a unicorn. None of us was deterred by being an "only" and probably few of us brought our "authentic selves" to the office, assuming we knew then or even now know what an authentic self is. Code–switching was routine, a way of life.

141

What we did was display a certain amount of that humility, worked extraordinarily hard and took advantage of the opportunities that came our way. Some might call that "luck."

Bonita—Automotive and Technology

I was recruited by Chrysler to head its Consumer Strategy team with no direct knowledge of the automotive industry. I had a rather tumultuous start advocating for the impending change in consumer expectations amid the acceleration of consumer–based technology, such as the personal computer and Internet access. The disruption was percolating and inevitable. It was during this time I had many innovative ideas that I felt would propel the industry forward and cement a consumer–first approach to car buying. It was also during this period during which the current head of Chrysler/Jeep pulled me aside and confided I may be right, but I could be more effective if I took a role one level below to learn the car business firsthand. He said I would still retain my executive compensation and perks. He offered to place me under the tutelage of one of his most admired leaders.

I had four choices: stay a bull in a china shop, suffer in career silence, leave the company or grab my humility and take his sage advice. After my inner voice said, "You've got this!" I jumped in with curiosity and my normal quest for achievement. I flourished in his organization running the Sebring brand and ultimately, after learning the entire vehicle life cycle of design, engineering, manufacturing and market launch, I moved upward to run the Dodge Car and Minivan brand team. For the auto industry, this was done within record speed–two years compared to those who had spent their entire careers at the company.

To this day, I cherish his wisdom and career brilliance for salvaging me from potential career self–sabotage. I often wondered about his path to the automotive executive ranks as a Jewish man. A study conducted in 1963 revealed "the auto industry's lagging employment of Jewish personnel. Of 51,000 white–collar, professional and executive employees in Detroit's Big Three auto companies at the time, only 328–less than three–fourths of one percent–were Jews."[74]

Within the tech industry, where meritocracy reigns, I experienced firsthand when "preparation meets opportunity" and when preparation meets an ally. When the selection process was underway for the leaders of the newly created multi–industry U.S. division at Google, it wasn't transparent if I was under consideration. The new president from our Europe, Middle East and Africa organization took a more personal yet structured approach. He had an initial meet and greet, which my colleagues told me was an informal chat. Nevertheless, I did my reconnaissance and found this leader never had an informal "chat." I came prepared with details about how my team planned to approach the auto industry on the dawn of an impending recession. Then he invited me and my husband to dinner with him and his wife. Later, I learned he reviewed the entire performance profiles of every single candidate, which includes self–assessments, peer reviews, development areas and ratings. Whew! Thank goodness I brought my nerdy, student self to the performance review process at Google. When someone asked how he selected the next leaders, he responded he read their entire file. While I was handed the most challenged industries (auto, finance, travel and media/entertainment) to lead, I was determined to provide a shining example to everyone on what "taking a chance" really means. We are always underestimated for our ability. Every ally who knows how to assess talent for women of color will be richly rewarded with results, resilience and everlasting respect.

Beverly Anderson—Banking

Beverly Anderson, president of the consumer division of a large credit reporting agency, was the keynote speaker at the Harvard Business School's Women's Student Association conference in February 2019. She related her very positive experience with her first white male boss.

In my adult life, my very first, real, non–family, non–professor sponsor was a senior executive, who happened to be a white male at what was then the Bank of Boston. He convinced me to join the company permanently after a successful internship during my junior year of college. He recognized that as a young African American woman working in corporate banking in the 1980s in Boston, far away from my Kentucky roots, this was going to be a big decision. He also understood that the bank's progress around diversity was in its infancy. He committed his support to us blazing trails together; he would demonstrate his support from the inside, and I would show up, do my best and perform at a level that would help prove the case. I knew I could say "yes" and he would uphold his commitment. I went on to have a very successful career at the bank and he went on to become the CEO.

The point I'm making is that we should be careful to avoid indicting an entire population of people because they are white men. We must be open to those who recognize and acknowledge our extraordinary brilliance and those who are bold in their advocacy and commitment to our success.

Jackie—Broadcast Journalism

Beverly's spirit of optimism was a constant in Jackie's story at CBS News.

Upon graduating from Harvard Business School, I was able to secure a job as the business and economics reporter for the CBS owned–and–operated station in Chicago, WBBM–TV. In the fall of 1978, I was paired with the health and medicine reporter. Together we offered viewers advice on "How to be Healthy and How to be Wealthy."

Less than a year in that position, I learned of an opening at the CBS Network News Washington, D.C. Bureau. I applied and was able to secure the spot. The team of reporters in the CBS D.C. Bureau was legendary – Dan Rather, Lesley Stahl, Fred Graham – the list goes on and on! I had admired all of them for decades, and now they were my colleagues. At that time, CBS News was known as the "Tiffany Network," the most brilliant gem among the then–Big 3 Networks–NBC, ABC and CBS. CNN had just been launched, and it would be years before it became the influential network it is now. Today's other cable giants, Fox News and MSNBC, were not part of the landscape.

On my first day, I met Brian Healy, a puckish Morning News senior producer. Irish Catholic to his core, he said something I've never forgotten; "Welcome to CBS News. You're going to have a wonderful career here." Years later, I asked Brian why he said that and what he had known about me before I arrived. He told me that he was impressed by my having attended Girls' Latin School for high school and Harvard. Both schools were proxies for my being smart. He added he felt a kinship with me that I didn't know about, a kinship I never would have imagined was meaningful.

145

I was from Boston, and he was from New Bedford, Massachusetts. That geographic convergence was enough for him to feel a bond with me.

Happily, Brian turned out to be right. Very quickly, I became a regular correspondent on his broadcast, covering the families of the men who were held hostage in Iran for 444 days. Within a few years, I was assigned to cover the presidential campaigns of Colorado Senator Gary Hart, then Reverend Jesse Jackson and finally, the first female candidate for vice president, Democratic Congresswoman Geraldine Ferraro. I was on the campaign trail for almost all of 1984, and during the Jackson campaign, I came to know a very talented cohort of African American reporters, photographers and camera people. I even married one, Gerald M. Boyd, whose final job at The New York Times *was managing editor.*

After the Democrats lost in November 1984, I was assigned to cover the Reagan White House. Gerald had the same assignment for the Times. *Together we traveled the world and spent weeks at the Santa Barbara White House. In 1988, we were both assigned to cover the George H. W. Bush campaign for president and then, the first year of the Bush–41 administration. We moved to New York when Gerald went into management and became an increasingly influential, Pulitzer Prize winning editor.*

My career flourished at the CBS News Northeast Bureau, based in New York. I called my beat, "mayhem and the arts." The people who count such things calculated I had more stories on the CBS Evening News with Dan Rather *in the early 1990s than any other African American female correspondent had ever had. I covered health news and criminal justice, including the trials of mass murderers Jeffrey Dahmer and Colin Ferguson. I won an Emmy Award for a* 48 Hours *broadcast about missing children. I covered*

146

a series of blockbuster French Impressionism exhibits and inter-viewed iconic 20th–century African American artists such as Elizabeth Catlett and Jacob Lawrence for the broadcast, CBS News Sunday Morning.

I had fun almost every day, but I quit after 22 years when I stopped having fun. I was approaching age 50. Television is not hospitable to most women as they age. Rather than fight or agree to be "ghettoized" in broadcasts other than the Evening News, *I decided it was time to trigger my MBA, my career insurance policy.*

Although there was a human resources department at CBS News, I don't recall ever having had a formal performance review, or a mentor or a sponsor. At one point during my White House years, I mentioned to the deputy bureau chief, a woman who shared my birthday and whom I felt was a real friend (Irish Catholic like Brian and a member of his same parish, if memory serves), that I felt overworked. Her reply was that if I didn't like the conditions, she could easily find someone else who could do my job. I never complained again.

Work was the coin of the realm. Work was the way you dealt with problems or setbacks. And every day was a new day. Something you might have done well on Monday was completely forgotten by Tuesday. But something that you may have screwed up was never forgotten.

Throughout all of my time at CBS News, I had only one African American boss, a Weekend News *executive producer. He was in charge of broadcasts only two days a week and held that job for just a short period. I did work with the occasional African American or Asian American producer. There was an assignment editor of color in D.C. and one in New York City. Many of the cameramen and soundmen were of color. A handful of videotape editors were African American.*

Yep, it was all pretty white!

In 2018, once Brian had retired, I asked him why he thought his prediction for my career so long ago had come true. His answers were instructive.

- *I was a good writer, so I could do the job without a lot of fuss or rewrites or extra work by Brian or other senior producers.*
- *I was perceived as attractive. I was tall. (How does anyone control for that?)*
- *I was energetic. Being perceived as "low energy" was apparently the kiss of death. Even 40 years later, Brian could still recall how difficult it was to work with low energy correspondents, primarily prickly, old, white men who had to be prodded or humored into actually doing any reporting.*
- *I had a sense of humor, a great smile and a hearty laugh.*
- *I was lucky enough to join the CBS Bureau in Washington when there was a lot of news during the Iran hostage crisis.*
- *Brian could use me because the more senior correspondents didn't want to work for the* CBS Morning News. *They preferred what was then perceived as the more prestigious* Evening News.

My being African American or a woman didn't figure into Brian's assessment. There were no diversity guidelines that I knew about during any of my time at CBS News.

Toward the end of our chat, I asked Brian if he had known about the nickname the cameramen had given me. Behind my back, they called me "Eleanor Roosevelt." They didn't intend it as a compliment, but I decided it was. And in the end, it was a protection.

For two decades, I traveled with and spent too much time in close quarters with scores of cameramen, soundmen and male producers—in cramped cars and airplanes and endless hotel rooms and press rooms. And yet, I was never harassed sexually. After all, Eleanor Roosevelt was hardly a glamour gal.

Brian said yes, he'd known about the nickname, but, God bless him. He thought the guys gave me the name because they perceived me as "having a sophistication that established a seriousness of purpose."

Working While They Watch

So, what are the lessons that today's women of color can draw from our experiences as well as those of the HBS alumnae featured in the profiles published as part of the 50th anniversary celebration of the African American Student Union?[75] How can one attract and keep the support of allies, especially white male allies?

1. Do exemplary work.
2. Listen. Become an excellent collaborator but also be able to do excellent work independently, so as not to need expensive or extensive supervision.
3. Know how to brand your work with the right "humble-brag" tone.
    a. Become known for being "high energy."
    b. Always act as if your glass is half–full. Having a positive attitude is an asset. Being known as a whiner is not.
    c. Become known as the person who sees a need and fills it before someone asks.
    d. Search out ways to be a driver of innovation.

4. Recognize that assimilating to your company's culture code is part of your job, as exhausting as it may be.

5. Your "authentic" self may not be your best or most appropriate self at work.

   a. Dress for the job you want, not necessarily the job you have.

   b. Life is long. Don't forget who you are. In an entrepreneurial environment or retirement, you can always be your best and most authentic self.

6. Learn how to center your grace. Sometimes this means being political, i.e., not calling out every microaggression every time you experience one.

7. Tap the GRATITUDE early and often.

8. Practice empathy. Often the white guys are even more afraid or insecure than you are.

9. Be on the constant lookout for allies, up and down the organizational chart.

10. Patience remains a virtue.

A Letter to Our White Male Allies

Dear Allies,

We see you. We've always seen you. We probably know more about you than you know about us. We are relentless and increasingly powerful, and we are on the march. Don't be afraid. We are YOUR allies too.

- Hire us.
  - At 24.3 million strong, Black women account for 14% of all U.S. women and 52% of all African Americans. Recent Nielsen data chronicles our steady growth

in population, income and educational attainment. Sixty-four percent of Black women in the United States agree their goal is to make it to the top of their professions; that's nearly double the percentage of non–Hispanic white women with the same goal.[76]

- Veer from your comfort zone.
- Express your gratitude and know that we will reciprocate. A simple note or expression of thanks can unleash a tsunami of positive feelings.
- Take a chance. Brilliance can come in different skin tones, different hair, from the introverted as well as the extroverted.
- We will make you proud.
- If we fail, we will listen and improve.[77]

Sincerely,

Your Future Leaders

P.S.

As a postscript to our letter, here are eight actions white male leaders can take that we have assembled from both our reading and our personal experiences:

- **Don't be afraid to ask questions.** It is difficult to step into someone else's shoes. You probably can't imagine how stressful it is to be the ONLY woman of color on a team. You probably would be surprised to learn what a microaggression feels like or how much time it takes to cope with or try to correct one. So ask. You can promote a safe, respectful and supportive work environment if you acknowledge and ask about what you don't currently know.

- **Pay attention to who is and is not attending company outings.** Women of color often opt out of social events and rarely share the personal details of their lives as openly as their white and male counterparts. Hobbies and weekend activities can and often do differ among the genders and races. If you are a manager and see this pattern, you could extend personal invitations to those who avoid office gatherings. You can make it clear you want to bring your female employees of color into your circle.

- **Listen better and offer praise.** Underrepresented minorities are called that for a reason. Women, and especially women of color, often feel invisible or over-looked at work. Several studies have found that Black women's statements were remembered less quickly and less accurately than those of their white female and male peers. Managers should make their staffs more aware of any unconscious or conscious biases and openly call it out whenever good work is being underappreciated or ignored. You should also highlight the contributions of these women through formal and informal communication channels, so the praise is on the record. And remember, even though women of color know their work is given extra scrutiny, they are still ambitious and committed to the work at hand.

- **Become comfortable feeling uncomfortable.** Providing timely, honest, yet critical feedback can be difficult – especially when there is an element of difference (race, gender, age) between the giver and receiver. To avoid any perception of being racist or sexist or ageist, managers often default to feedback that reflects "protective hesitation" rather than the candor women of color need in order to grow and develop their skills. Instead of giving in to your fears, managers should embrace opportunities to deliver feedback in a manner that shows they care deeply about their employees' personal growth and advancement.

- **Look for potential, not perfection.** We have all seen the stories about men feeling qualified with just a handful of the relevant skill sets and women feeling inadequate, even when they are overqualified. Now often called "people," executives have to trust their instincts about who can and cannot be an effective leader, based on her past experiences and qualifications. Too often, though, women of color can be excluded from a pool of candidates because they may not have been given the same opportunities as their white and male colleagues. So, it's important to also widen the candidate pool by recruiting and assessing for potential in addition to past performance. There are tools available to organizations that can evaluate curiosity, insight, engagement and determination, qualities that are seen as leading indicators of future competence in leadership roles.
- **Bias is real.** While 42% of companies check for bias in reviews and promotions by gender, only 18% track outcomes for the compounding bias of race and gender. Tracking the performance of women of color as well as the velocity and the rate at which they're

hired and promoted versus their peers is the only way to measure progress in creating a more diverse leadership bench.

- **Ask why.** Exit interviews are one source of rich anecdotal data on the effectiveness of diversity and inclusion programs. But very few companies offer a mandatory exit interview policy for diverse employees. Honest conversations with departing women of color can generate new ideas about how to improve the overall employee experience before talent walks out the door. If HR doesn't take up this cause, managers can do it themselves, informally.

- **Just get started.** A quarter of chief diversity officers say they still have to make the business case for diversity. Some boards of directors are admitting they are honestly tired of hearing about inclusion. Promoting and building trusting relationships with people whose lives and experiences may be unlike yours is hard work, but this work is essential to harness the potential of an undeniably diversifying workforce.

Make no mistake. We understand that none of these steps — for women of color or for their white male allies — is easy. But all of them are necessary. Change is coming, one way or another.

A case in point: in 2019, in the aftermath of a series of high–profile firings of white male leaders at CBS News driven by the #MeToo movement, the News Division is now led by Susan Zirinsky, its first white female president. Her top three deputies are women of color. The undisputed star of *CBS This Morning* is Gayle King and the anchor of the *CBS Evening News* is Norah O'Donnell. In a year or so, it will be interesting to see if and how the power dynamics change within the organization.

In life and in our careers, we are glass–half–full women. We have always found that we are enough–for ourselves and in our workplaces. But as we've said, being "the onlys," being "sole sisters" has created physical and psychological challenges. In our next chapter, we will explore those and offer some remedies.

 **LIVING LOG**

❑ Do you have "allies" at work? What are their race or gender? Are they the same as yours?

❑ Do you have "sponsors" at work?

❑ Do you have "mentors" at work? Do you have mentors in your real life?

❑ How would you define each of these roles? Is there any overlap in the roles?

❑ How well do you really know your colleagues? What are their insecurities?

❑ How can you "serve" your allies, sponsors or mentors? What can YOU do to make their lives better, to make them identify with you?

❑ What can YOU do to make someone want to help you pursue/achieve your career goals?

❑ Do you think you are paid the same as others with your skills and job title? If not, how would you go about redressing the differentials?

❑ Are you an optimist or a pessimist?

❑ What does it take to do the job you have with excellence?

❑ What does it take to do the job you want with excellence?

❑ How can you make sure your excellence is perceived and rewarded?

❑ How would you define "white privilege?" Do you think it can ever be eliminated or equalized?

❑ What are the sources of YOUR privilege?

❑ Have you been given honest feedback about your work, even if it made you uncomfortable?

❑ Have you ever asked for feedback when you knew it was warranted?

Chapter Six

Women @ Work +

Much of this book has been about leadership, careers and triumphing over perceived or real obstacles. With new, disruptive technologies opening unexpected fields, we see women of all colors exhibiting the confidence needed to explore and find both their passions and their purpose. Reading through the comments of the Gen Z women in our survey, *Women of Color in Business: Cross Generational Survey©*, we were excited to see so many in our youngest cohort pursuing careers in fields as diverse as zoology and orthodontics as well as education and the STEM fields of computer science and applied mathematics.

We have called this chapter Women@Work+ because we're going to shift gears a bit and focus on the +, the plus part of being a woman who works and the guidance we need to prosper.

In December 2019, U.S. Labor Department data showed that for the first time in a decade, the share of women on payrolls, excluding farmworkers and the self–employed, exceeded the share of men. Women held 50.04% of jobs, surpassing men on payrolls by 109,000.[78]

That percentage provides context for another important statistic. According to Women's Policy Research, half of all households with children under 18 in the U.S. have a breadwinner mother, who is either a single mother heading the household, irrespective of earnings, or a married mother who provides at least 40 percent of the couple's joint earnings.

This situation varies significantly by ethnicity: 81.1% of Black mothers are breadwinners, with 60.9% of Black mothers raising families on their own. There are three times as many single Black mother breadwinners as there are married Black mother breadwinners.[79]

In the *Harvard Business School Spheres of Influence Alumni Survey*, only 61% of the Black women respondents indicated they were married/partnered compared to 78% for Black men and 82% for white women. Only 45% of HBS Black women have children versus 71% for white women and 80+% for Black men. The authors of the HBS survey warned the data about women with children might be skewed because so many of the respondents were relatively younger alumnae. Nonetheless, we are among the majority of HBS Black alumnae who have never had children.[80]

Did we miss much by not becoming mothers physically? Speaking for ourselves, the answer is no. We were moving fast. Collectively, however, the women in our generation of HBS Black alumnae have fulfilled the "mother" role in traditional and myriad non–traditional ways.

Michelle Morris Weston—Traditional Mothering

From the outside, Michelle Morris Weston has the life we all desire: a strong 32–year marriage to an accomplished attorney, a thriving career at a major financial services firm and two successful adult children. In 2020, her son graduated from HBS as a Baker Scholar, an honor reserved for those in the top 10% of the class. He has an exciting job waiting at a leading, global, private investment firm. Her daughter is also on Wall Street, working as an equity research associate for a major firm. How did Michelle achieve it all? "I believed in myself and prayed a lot."

In high school, I was accustomed to being the only Black girl in advanced math and honors English. I put pressure on myself to be three times as good all the time, to be viewed as a valued member of any team.

Thirty-five years out of HBS, I am aware that I am still the only woman of color most of the time in meetings, both internally in my firm as well as externally. The onus was always on me to make colleagues, managers and clients feel comfortable. But I had a gift of having grown up in a family structure and a community in which my self—worth was validated. Good friends and relationships and my faith were counterweights to the energy that was required to thrive in a tough business environment.

Today I feel blessed and lucky because yes, my kids are moving on the right path, are good people and have strong values. Looking back, even as a full—time working mother, I felt I had a stark choice of prioritizing my family or career trajectory; I joyfully chose to prioritize my family.

When both children were in diapers, both under age five, I was traveling non—stop. After a year of this, I said, "I'm not happy. I need a break! I don't want to travel until both of my children are in school full—time." And that meant I had to take a lateral move into a new job.

Even when my children were older, when they would arrive home from school at 3:30 p.m., they would fax their math questions to me, and I would have a "secret" call with them at 4 or 4:30 p.m. I went into "stealth mode" to connect with my kids because my work environment did not have any other working mothers, and the business culture didn't acknowledge issues involving working mothers.

There were no role models — no other full–time working mothers at the VP level — and I was the only Black officer level professional who was a full–time working mother. It was so liberating when I heard another HBS Black alum (another mother of two) say at a conference that if she had to take one of her children to a pediatrician appointment, she would just do it. I felt that I had to ask for permission to take time off when my children needed their vaccinations. I frequently got pushback for taking that time.

What sustained me was that every Sunday, we would go to church as a family. My husband was very involved; my children attended Sunday school and stayed engaged with youth church programs throughout high school; their spiritual foundation was a priority. They now tell me that they are grateful for their connection to God, to something greater than themselves. And they appreciate all of the lessons that my husband and I tried to give them. The three main ones were 1) work to your potential and move the bar up every year 2) continue to challenge yourself and be a life–long learner and 3) give back to your community, be a role model and mentor children of color who will benefit from you believing in their potential.

Depelsha McGruder—Moms of Black Boys United

In 2020, Depelsha McGruder received the prestigious John Whitehead Award for Social Enterprise from the Harvard Business School Club of New York City. (Both Jackie and Bonita have been actively involved with this alumni club as members of the board.) The honor celebrated Depelsha's creation of two organizations dedicated to positively influencing how Black boys and men are perceived and treated by law enforcement and in society. This work is entirely separate from her day job as a senior executive at a major foundation, but it is critically important to her job as the mother of two Black sons.

It started accidentally. In July 2016, there were two murders of Black men by police covered on national television, Alton Sterling and Philando Castile. I was in the airport in Atlanta, and the shooting of Alton Sterling by a Baton Rouge police officer was shown at close range, over and over again. The broadcasts paralyzed me.

The next morning, a Thursday, I turned on CNN again, and a different family was on the news, this time in Minnesota. The police shooting of Philando Castile was practically broadcast live on Facebook, with his girlfriend and her four–year–old daughter in the car. I couldn't get out of bed. I didn't go to work. I thought about my sons and the fact that we have to teach Black boys from a young age to be afraid and comply completely if they have an encounter with the police. I thought of the mothers of Michael Brown and Trayvon Martin and Eric Garner and so many others that came before them.

I had to make breakfast for my sons. As I was scrambling eggs and cooking turkey sausage, I typed Mothers of Black boys and created a group on Facebook. I sent it to the first 30 people whom I could think of who had Black sons. Five minutes later, by the time I finished cooking breakfast, the number in the FB group had grown to 500. I didn't really know how FB groups were organized or that random people could just add other people. Within 12 hours, we had more than 21,000 moms from all across the country who had joined. We now have more than 170,000.

Within two days, we had people offering to make T-shirts and wanting to plan a conference and start local chapters. We changed the name to Moms of Black Boys United and got a trademark and a URL. The ideas snowballed. I was nervous and unsure of how to proceed, but my best friend Otesa encouraged me and asked, "Who is better equipped to do this than you? If not now, when? If not you, who?"

A mother in North Carolina named Crys Baldwin posted in the group, "Let's plan a conference call for 7:30 a.m. on Saturday." 50 plus moms were on that call two days after the group started. People wanted to plan a march, but I said I'm not a marcher. Let's develop a long–term strategy. We set up a steering committee and had conference calls every Saturday morning. I crafted a vision and mission statement with five pillars and we decided to set up two sister organizations.

One of the organizations, a 501 (c) (3), Moms of Black Boys United, Inc., provides information and support for moms of Black sons and promotes positive images of Black boys and men. It is dedicated to changing perceptions, encouraging self–care and fostering understanding of the plight of Black boys and men in America by telling their stories, celebrating their accomplishments and connecting them to opportunities.

The other organization, a 501 (c) (4), which now has 14 chapters, M.O.B.B. United for Social Change, Inc. (MUSC) is the advocacy arm. Its goal is to influence policy at the federal, state and local levels to ensure that Black boys and men are treated fairly and equitably. MUSC is focused on eradicating harassment, brutality and unwarranted use of deadly force by law enforcement.

Overall, my vision is to train moms to be effective advocates for their sons and for themselves in every situation, and for us to be the most comprehensive resource for moms and sons on navigating all of the situations that our sons may face in society.

A Patchwork of Mothers

In the Black community, we say we have mothers "everywhere." Sisters, aunts, cousins, godmothers and grandmothers all play — and have always played — prominent roles in our lives. Some of us even adopt a "mothering" pose at work. The goal of all these mothers is to help our youngsters grow and thrive. The challenge ahead is how, whether and when the young people ask for that help.

Bonita—Mothers Everywhere

You never know the impact you can have on someone either directly or indirectly. I've found as you ascend, you can either close the door or open the door wider. Time with others is my way of giving back the time others shared with me. Your leadership style is shaped by those you meet along the way.

Debbie Allen (star of the movie Fame, *actress, dancer, entrepreneur, producer) said it best when I interviewed her for my Howard University newspaper,* The Hilltop, *in 1977. In my story, "Dancer Returns Home," Debbie called the upward climb to stardom "a little scary." She then added, more importantly, she didn't want to hold it all by herself. "I want to bring my people with me." She went on to stress the importance of remembering prestige, power and money should not overcome the development of one's cultural community."*

Debbie told me as a Black woman, she feels a "great deal of commitment and obligation, because there are many coming behind and more still to come."

Her success today is a marvelous one, and she has brought so many along, including me. In 2019, I attended the Leading

Women Defined conference, which gathers senior Black women executives across multiple industries. As part of the event, a dance class with Debbie Allen was a special enrichment activity. I gleefully participated as the entire class moved in Fame–style energy and harmony. Little did she know the impact she had on me as a Hilltop *reporter and Howard University undergraduate.*

Jackie calls her young friends her "chicks" and welcomes them "clustering under my wings." She is reassured by their hopefulness. In response to her dismay about the recent rollbacks of progress in civil and women's rights in the U.S. and globally, these "chicks" have consistently told Jackie that THEY will fix these issues, once and for all!

In return, she has encouraged several in their entrepreneurial and political ventures, sometimes making investments and/or campaign contributions. She often hosts wide–ranging brunch and dinner discussions with the chicks, connecting those who may not know each other. Also, she has sometimes attempted (and once succeeded) at matchmaking. She also encourages memberships in organizations like the Council on Foreign Relations as well as affiliate groups aimed at young people and people of color within major New York City cultural organizations (e.g., the Frederick Douglass Council of the New–York Historical Society, the Friends of Education of the Museum of Modern Art, the Young Patrons Circle of the Alvin Ailey American Dance Theater, as well as evening classes at the Juilliard School).

Help When Getting Ahead

We asked the 4,005 respondents in our *Women of Color in Business: Cross Generational Survey©* to name their sources of career support. Family topped the list for Black and LatinX women. Asian and white women said they rely more on their peers and supervisors at work.

Career Advancement: How important have each of the following been to you in helping you get ahead in your career?

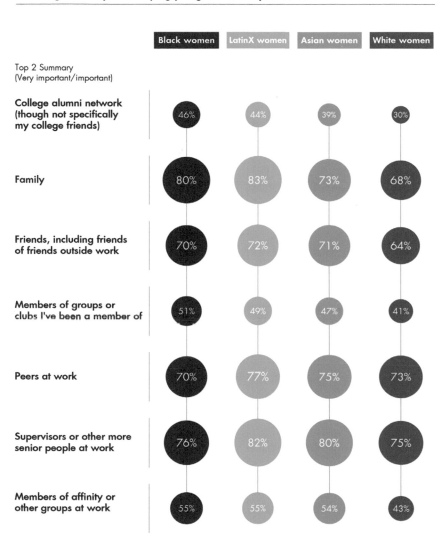

Top 2 Summary
(Very important/important)

	Black women	LatinX women	Asian women	White women
College alumni network (though not specifically my college friends)	46%	44%	39%	30%
Family	80%	83%	73%	68%
Friends, including friends of friends outside work	70%	72%	71%	64%
Members of groups or clubs I've been a member of	51%	49%	47%	41%
Peers at work	70%	77%	75%	73%
Supervisors or other more senior people at work	76%	82%	80%	75%
Members of affinity or other groups at work	55%	55%	54%	43%

Women of Color in Business: Cross Generational Survey©

We took a closer look at the variety of sources of career support that our youngest Gen Z women are seeking, and we contrasted those with the sources we Boomer women relied on. The findings were most striking when we compared Black and white women.

The youngest women— Black and white—say in record numbers they plan to turn to their "mothers in the office" for coaching and inspiration, i.e., their supervisors or more senior people at work. They are relying on their peers and their families. Affinity groups and college alumni networks are further down on their lists.

By contrast, we older Black women have relied much more on our families for support. Supervisors and friends come next. But affinity and alumni groups are way down on our lists.

Boomer white women are looking to their predominantly white supervisors and their peers. Friends and family are further down. The findings hint at a trend we're seeing anecdotally among younger Millennial and Gen X workers of all colors; they are seeking help from new categories of allies and mentors. They include executive coaches as well as mental and physical health professionals. Here are two examples:

- One of Jackie's "chicks" received a referral for a therapist when he mentioned how much stress he was under to a colleague at an affinity group for entrepreneurs. The group calls itself "Scotchreprenuers." Started in 2013, their concept is pretty simple. Passionate, entrepreneurial folks get together to chat and drink the finest brands of scotch, all for a nominal fee of $30 per event. And yes, this is primarily a group frequented by young men.

- In early 2019, Bonita was the guest speaker at a somewhat similar gathering called Fortune & Forks. (She brought Jackie along as her wing–woman). The dinner was one of a series of events aimed at cultivating a community of young, ambitious women of color who embody the spirit of what it takes to thrive in various industries. These 2017 and 2018 college graduates asked questions about careers in technology and the media as well as tips for self–care. They are the embodiment of "sisters doing it for themselves."

In fact, in our interviews with several young executives — some Harvard B School alums and many not — we found examples and explanations for the new focus on multiple sources of outside career help.

- *You need a community of people whom you can ask questions of, a safe place. It's a real shock though when you get out and realize there is racism in the real world.*
- *Find your people and your "tribe." You need a sounding board of women who can relate to you and keep you sane. Be a resource for them, too.*
- *Be kind to yourself. Being a Black woman in corporate America is exhausting. It can take a toll on your mental health, having to prove yourself next to a white person. Don't ignore the gym or your family. Put yourself first from a mental health and wellness perspective.*

- *You need a personal board of directors to give you a wide–angle and a longitudinal view. In your 20s, you're responding to the opportunities that are coming in. Become a VP, go to B school, become an entrepreneur. There's an unending number of options, but you need people to pressure test these options.*
- *Strive for work/life integration. At my digital media company, I was getting hosed by the engineers because I didn't know how to code as well as they did. So, I signed up for Code Academy so I could kick their butts. If you're on a growth trajectory, you should learn what you don't know.*
- *Keep yourself healthy. If you burn out at age 27, no one will be impressed. Figure out, for example, if you get sad when it's dark outside. Get control of yourself because YOU are your moneymaker!*

The inescapable conclusion is that these younger women (and men) have learned something we Boomers didn't or couldn't experience—the need to ask for help, help from inside your organization, help from career coaches and mental health professionals, help from peers. Always, always ask for help!

We can't rewrite history, but we Boomers can help those who seek our wisdom. We can find comfort in our toughness and strength. And we can find new sources of power in perhaps the final acts of our careers.

Unleashed Power—Motherhood and Menopause

We have talked about various forms of motherhood, but let's change gears and discuss menopause. It's still a topic that makes many people feel queasy. But for those of us who have or are about to experience it, menopause is fabulous, liberating, a secret weapon, a way to unleash our power.

In a recent *Financial Times* column called "How Older Women are Trying to Change the World," scholar Anne–Marie Slaughter dubbed menopause "phase three of life...a time to take risks and upset apple carts." This book is at the core of Bonita's and Jackie's phase three–our time to give back, to make a difference, to come together to pay forward the successes we have experienced. This project is also a warning for the young: You don't have to do everything now! Save some of your goals and objectives for later. As long as you're alive, there can still be new ideas, more mountains to climb, more greatness to experience and more good to give.

Slaughter cites Harvard economists Claudia Goldin and Lawrence Katz who published a study in 2017 that shows 28% of women aged 65 to 69 were still in the paid workforce, as were 16% of women aged 70 to 74. The percentages were double the comparable numbers some 40 years ago. Historian Susan Mattern, author of *The Slow Moon Climbs: The Science, History, and Meaning of Menopause*, posits that high productivity and zero reproductivity for half of the population are good for the economy and for society.[81]

Jackie's Story—If You're No Longer a Girl...

Many people thought I had lost my mind when I quit CBS News at the age of 50. I did find solace when I saw a few other women abandoning high-profile careers for what – an adventure, a break from stress, a chance to learn and experience something new. For me, it was a chance to walk away from something familiar but increasingly painful. Happily, several of those women introduced me to foreign policy and education non-profits such as the Off-the-Record Lecture Series of the Foreign Policy Association and the HBS African-American Alumni Association. The friendships that I made as a result sustain me to this day.

In hindsight, I can see that I quit CBS News, in part, because of the liberating effects of menopause. If I was no longer a "girl," I didn't have to pretend to be a good one. I could take big risks. I could redefine what "enough" income meant. I no longer had to rely on bosses' or men's assessments of my "likeability" or "sexual attractiveness." I could still learn things, specifically how to be a consultant. And in my new role, I could hire and fire clients. I decided to work only with and for people whom I liked. In short, I didn't have to put up with internal politics, or accept a level of mediocrity that I found disappointing, or smile or wink or ignore obvious injustices or poor decision making by higher-ups, just to make a living.

I hadn't realized how numb I had been for decades, but menopause allowed me to begin the process of unthawing, of feeling my feelings. The feelings were so powerful, they were impossible to ignore.

Those feelings gave me, give me power! I don't care what others think. I only care what I think. And what's the worst that can happen? What is anyone going to do to an "old lady?" Whatever it is, bring it on! I've survived worse.

I did talk with various friends before I made my major career transition, and several were instrumental in helping me make that change. But the process was totally ad hoc.

Times have changed, happily. Today, we advise our Millennial and Gen Z workers to plan their career moves with more precision. And today, we are offering our daughters and younger sisters a framework that we call Teaming Up.

 **LIVING LOG**

❑ How many "mothers" are in your experience?
❑ How can/should a Black parent successfully raise her/his children in 21st century America?
❑ What is the role of faith in raising children?
❑ What did YOUR parents do to guide and advise you in your career?
❑ Do you seek help plotting your career? From whom? Has the source of that help changed in recent years?
❑ In your spare time, what sorts of organizations do you join? What kind have you started?

Chapter Seven

Winning

When we were accepted into Harvard Business School and matriculated, we won. And so did the almost 700 Black and Latinx women who have ever attended HBS.

In total, the school's Black graduates number about 2,300, slightly less than 4% of all alumni. But African American women represent 35% of all Black graduates between 1969 and 2017–an outsized percentage compared to 27% for women overall among HBS graduates during the same time period. This overrepresentation of Black women is part of a national trend in higher education. "According to the Council of Graduate Schools, 69% of blacks enrolled in all graduate programs are women. In every graduate degree program, women outnumber men, except in elite MBA programs."[82]

So, we beat the odds for women overall as well as for Black women in elite MBA programs. And we did it by following in the footsteps of Lillian Lincoln Lambert.

Lillian has written poignantly about her alone–ness, her physical and cultural isolation on campus, but she didn't suffer in silence. She teamed up with the handful of Black male students on campus to insist the HBS administration actively recruit more students of color. Together, they launched the HBS African American Student Union and were honored for their work at a special celebration marking the 50th anniversary of the founding of AASU in 2018. We are the beneficiaries of Lillian's leadership.

Yes, she and we are leaders. Yes, we are role models. And, like Lillian, we are determined to share what we know and what we've learned with the goal of expanding our numbers, our power and our influence.

What is the secret sauce? In a nutshell, know your craft. Know yourself. Know others. Know the difference between power and freedom. Know when to move on. No matter which industry sector you examine, you can find "Black girl magic" — women of color crushing the opposition, thriving, succeeding as never before. Yes, there remain a number of tragic glass–half–empty statistics, but there are so many, many glass–half–full stats.

What a Difference Four Centuries Can Make

Almost every day, we see evidence of women of color knocking down barriers, demonstrating over and over again that they — we — are clearly "more than." The stories inspire and validate our strength, resilience and unlimited futures in any field we might choose to enter. Here is just a sampling:

- In May 2019, West Point graduated its largest number of Black female graduates. Granted, there were only 34 of them; granted, they represented just 3.58 percent of the total 950 graduates. But still, this is an undeniable benchmark for physically and mentally strong women, ready for command and control.[83]

- In the same month, another barrier fell. All of America's beauty queens—Miss America, Miss Teen USA and Miss USA —were women of color some 35 years after Vanessa Williams was crowned the first Black woman to be Miss America.[84] In December, the fourth crown, Miss Universe, went to a Black woman, Zozibini Tunzi of South Africa.[85]

- In August 2019, gymnast Simone Biles was called "the greatest athlete of all time" after dominating the U.S. Gymnastics championship, winning her sixth all–around title. Biles seemed to levitate as she flawlessly executed the most difficult floor and bar exercises ever attempted. And yet, a few weeks later, to deter other gymnasts from trying skills they are not physically capable of doing, the International Gymnastics Federation watered down the value of a new element Biles planned to perform at the world championships. "Am I in a league of my own? Yes. But that doesn't mean you can't credit me for what I'm doing," Biles complained after learning of the decision by the women's technical committee. Despite the controversy, Biles routed the competition and cemented her status as the World Championships' most decorated gymnast ever. In total, she has won 25 career world championship medals, the most among women and men. She also had two more signature moves named after her, an honor that is awarded only after an athlete submits the move for consideration and successfully lands it in a major competition.[86]

- In early September 2019, women of color dominated the U.S. Open tennis tournament. A few days after a sculpture of Althea Gibson was unveiled in honor of her having broken the sport's color line in the early 1950s, Naomi Osaka, Coco Gauff, Sloane Stephens, Madison Keys, Taylor Townsend and of course, Venus and Serena Williams, all played their hearts out. During the tournament, "Coco craziness" broke out as fans cheered her everywhere, from homes to sports bars. The older legends played against Coco with some losing and some winning. Throughout the week, however, this band of Black "unicorns" showcased its collective power and attendant blessings. These Black tennis players forever changed an entire sport. As we sat in front of our televisions, we cheered this "blessing," this gathering of unicorns, this convocation soaring high and above.
- In late November 2019, the New York City Ballet announced a first. The company selected 11–year old Charlotte Nebress to perform the role of Marie in the holiday performances of "George Balanchine's *The Nutcracker*. The classic production dates back to 1954, but this was the first time that a Black dancer had been chosen to perform the leading role.[87]
- In 2020, the American Ballet Theater announced it would feature Misty Copeland and Calvin Royal III as the first Black couple starring in *Romeo and Juliet*.
- In U.S. politics, the power and influence of women of color have been acknowledged. Yes, there has been a spike in the numbers of women of color running

for office and winning their elections. Yes, California Senator Kamala Harris' bid for the Democratic presidential nomination may not have succeeded, but researchers are finding that increasingly, women of color are turning out to vote, mobilizing their communities and thereby driving change in U.S. politics.

o Since 2008, women of color have grown by 18% in the general population, but by 25% among registered voters.

o In the 2018 midterm elections, 30 million more people voted than in 2014. For women of color, the increased turnout was 37%; for Latinas, it was 51%; and for Asian American and Pacific Islander women, 48%.

- Democrats seem to have been the primary beneficiaries. Ninety–three percent of Black women voters supported a Democratic House candidate as did 68% of Native American women, 76% of Latinas and 73% of Asian–American and Pacific Islander women.[88]

We have cited the data about the spike in Black female entrepreneurs. They, too, are achieving more and more against still formidable obstacles.

Amanda E. Johnson—Mented Cosmetics

The story of Mented Cosmetics is still being written. But three years in, we're looking pretty good. We want to be the everyday home for beauty.

That's an understatement. Amanda E. Johnson and her fellow Harvard Business School alumna co–founder, KJ Miller, personally experienced a "pain point" common to most Black women, finding makeup shades perfectly pigMENTED to match their skin tones. So they created their own vegan, paraben–free, non–toxic and cruelty–free lipsticks, followed by additional products for the face and eyes as well as brushes.

In April 2018, they were among the 26 Black female founders whom *Vanity Fair* magazine assembled for a photoshoot and declared "the most visible faces of a revolution." All had raised more than $1 million in outside funding.[89]

By November 2019, Amanda Johnson and KJ Miller were offering other female entrepreneurs advice about starting businesses in *The New York Times*. "The world truly does work on a 'who you know' basis, and even in the best intentions, people invest in and want to work with people who look like them, talk like them, have similar experiences, Ms. Johnson said."[90]

In January 2020, they launched a bi–monthly series of appearances selling seven bundles of products nationwide on QVC and HSN as well as QVC.com and HSN.com.

If our physical products are relevant in 10 years, if Mented Cosmetics is a household name, then I'll say that we've been a success. We know that we're riding a boom. The demand for beauty products among Black women has always been there. But now, venture capitalists want to diversify their portfolios and have a winning media narrative, and we are the beneficiaries. But the expectations of this startup machine are huge! Now, no one can be just an analyst. Everyone has to be a contributing member on Day 1. And so your leadership techniques have to change. The pressure and expectations for performance and critical thinking skills are all huge.

Leading While Black

When you see so many examples of women of color in leadership roles, it's easy to forget how new this phenomenon is, and of course, we tend to block out or want to forget the rampant misogyny, the mansplaining, the verbal, psychological and in some cultures, the legal and physical assaults against women.

What are the hallmarks, the guideposts of "leading while Black?" We have talked with a number of our Harvard Business School colleagues, examined our personal careers and have come to a series of conclusions. Leading while Black does require a certain amount of code–switching, of restraining one's natural exuberance, of practicing a tremendous amount of diplomacy. At times, it may even require bringing along a white man to a meeting as a metaphorical and physical security blanket for the "less woke" participants in a meeting. Yes, it's unfair that you may need a white man in your corner, but if you recognize that you are employing this tactic as a deliberate strategy, we can think of it as a form of "winning."

Kimberly Foster—Being the First

Not everyone is coming from diverse or inclusive backgrounds. I assume that, for a lot of people, having a Black peer or boss in the workplace is a foreign concept. I may very well be the first one whom they have encountered to date.

Certain stereotypes do exist about Black people and/or Black women, so know what you're up against. Don't change who you are, but just know how certain reactions can be perceived. Some

178

may argue to be the complete opposite of said stereotypes, but others (like myself) think it's a shame to completely dim your light because others may think it's too bright.

I am not sure if I change my leadership style when working with non–Black people (I don't like to code–switch too much because I think it's exhausting), but I definitely am a little more formal and organized when I'm leading a group of non–Black people. I want to be on top of my game.

Depelsha McGruder—Authenticity

Depelsha McGruder doesn't think much about her race–or any race–when she's leading. What she focuses on is authenticity, showing up as who she is.

You have to be comfortable in your own skin, which conveys confidence. If people see you are comfortable with yourself, it puts them at ease and enables them to trust you more, regardless of the race of the people you're managing.

For those whom my comfort with myself causes discomfort, I view that as their problem, not mine. I don't internalize other people's discomfort with me as a Black woman. As I said in a speech recently, I feel that I belong wherever I go. If anyone is uncomfortable with me being in a room, they are welcome to leave the room.

Depelsha emphasized another distinctive element in her leadership style. She listens more than she talks, especially when she's the person making the final decision.

I may enter a room with a point of view, but I always want to incorporate the views of others. Some leaders have to always dominate the conversation. But I say, why not listen to everyone in the room? I don't have to influence the person making the decision when it's ME!

Bring Your Best Self

If you talk to anyone from HBS, they will tell you to strut your best work. Today, it's commonplace to hear that we should be able to bring our "whole self" to work. Depelsha describes this phenomenon as "authenticity." To be honest, we both think we can be authentic and bring our unique selves to work as long as it's our "best" self, i.e., bringing our best work and our best proposition to whatever workplace we are in.

Every workplace has a culture that should be studied before you join. From the day Bonita set foot in the Google office, she could sense the campus feel: intellectual engagement, collaboration, curiosity, mission–driven, etc. It was the fabled Googley. In every fashion, it was the polar opposite of the corporate work environments that she had experienced in the past. The automotive industry was hierarchical and, in every aspect, top–down from the reserved executive parking to the executive dining rooms and executive wing. On the other hand, the original information technology field had a paternalistic legacy where everyone stuck around well beyond their "expiration dates."

Bonita—Taking The Road Less Travelled

My journey of leadership seems to entail two consistent and notable themes. I haven't always followed the "cool crowd" and I've searched for new trails in the forest.

Upon leaving business school, most of my classmates followed the siren call (and the big money) into consulting and investment banking. I had chosen business school over law school because I was determined to learn how to run a company. I decided early on that my framework for leadership would center around the combination of strategy plus in–depth operating skills. Most people can manage themselves or even small teams. However, it takes different qualities to lead others at scale with commitment and clarity of vision.

Unlike Jackie's experience, where babysitting was discouraged, I found babysitting to be my first step toward being a leader — practicing with youngsters over whom I had a degree of assigned control. While I don't have children myself, I love being around the youthful spirit of creativity, defiance, energy, innovation and resilience. With my little minions, I learned the nuances of power and commands (e.g., "It's time to go to bed") versus influence (e.g., "Let's go to bed, and I'll read your favorite story").

My first element of defiance was to choose, in the mid–seventies, to attend a historically Black college over the suggestions of some high school friends who urged me to apply to one of the Ivy League women's colleges. Growing up in the Midwest, in Denver, I knew I was missing something in my soul. As much as I tried to absorb my African American roots, I still grew up in a world of 10%, the representation of African Americans in Denver at the time. Moving to Washington, D.C. the "Chocolate City," was dazzling and, in many respects, what we call in tech, being "uncomfortably excited." I was internally uncomfortable in my new environment, yet thrilled with the possibilities of absorbing the full education of being in our nation's capital.

I offer my sincerest gratitude to Howard for opening the aperture to my vision of leadership with folks who represented the beauty and intellect of the mosaic across all U.S. regions (North, South, East, West) as well as the African Diaspora and the Caribbean. Howard was my yellow brick road and sandbox combined.

My head was spinning when I arrived, and my pride grew immensely when I saw I was surrounded by future Black doctors, lawyers, engineers, architects, dentists, artists, and business professionals. Every dimension was covered. It was at Howard that my leadership journey genuinely began. Little did I realize many years later, that Howard truly gave me superpowers. Attending Howard made me stronger and more purposeful. The school has a legacy of leadership, and combined with my Harvard Business School degree, it was a double H.

Howard gave me confidence while HBS opened many doors as an Ivy League stamp of approval. Indeed, a 2014–2015 Gallup poll found that 58% of HBCU students responded positively to the question: "my professors at my university cared about me as a person." The number was just 25% for non–historically Black college students. The poll also found two other positive outcomes for HBCU students: stronger wellbeing for purpose (51% of HBCU students responded positively versus 43% for non–HBCUs) as well as financial wellbeing (40% versus 29%).[91]

Winning at the Beginning

Like Bonita, Amanda E. Johnson flourished during her undergraduate career at Howard University. Her internships with a major investment bank and a luxury brand prepared her well for full–time jobs at three prestigious companies in finance, media and retailing before she ventured off into her successful start–up career at Mented Cosmetics.

I was great at my job, whatever it was. I always got the highest ranking among my peers in investment banking, because I knew how that world worked. There's a corporate hierarchy, and you have to understand both the structure and how you fit into it. You have to be able to manage up, down and sideways. You have to be pragmatic and perfect the ways that you communicate within the "machine." I loved the experience of mastering the fundamentals of critical thinking and teamwork and communications. You have to learn fast and exceed expectations no matter the team that you're on.

You must find champions or mentors who can explain the "machine," that it's not a meritocracy. I had my first, best and most honest mentors when I was at Howard.

Winning in the Muddy Middle

When you hit the middle of your career, it gets hard. It becomes the muddy middle. You can either continue to ascend or plateau. It's during the middle when you must learn career finesse. For women of color, this plateau may prove especially problematic. Often, our parents taught us to put our heads down. Their typical advice was: "That's the route to getting promoted." That's what they had to do, just work hard. But things are different now.

Now, one needs to focus on getting a corporate sponsor, meeting the right people, in addition, of course, to doing an excellent job. While learning how the game is played, one of Jackie's mentees in the media field revealed that she had gotten knocked down a few times.

A more senior person told me that I had to spend more time on the executive floor. I said that I had real work to do. But he said, go into the executive vice president's office and tell him what you're working on. My male and female white counterparts—call them Bob and Susie — were touting their work, and they were perceived as rock stars, while I was grinding away at my desk.

Exposure allows you to rise. Know how to toot your own horn, but do it authentically. The mentee learned that "Bob and Susie got promoted because they knew how to promote themselves!" Bonita calls this strategy "the finesse of the humblebrag."

Here are additional tips for winning in the muddy middle.

- Show up. Take advantage of everything — e.g., industry conferences, after–work social hours, events that your various alumni organizations hold, internal town halls. You never know whom you'll meet or what opportunity will present itself.
- Become known for your value add. Be a giver.
- Ask questions and make connections.
- Focus on ensuring credit is given where credit is due. Know how to "promote" your work upward and across the organization.
- Sometimes the fastest way up is across. Lateral moves early in your career can give you a breadth of experience that will pay dividends later. Don't be afraid to take that lateral move before you figure out exactly where you belong in an organization.
- In today's age of social media, it is important to have a personal brand and recognizable profile. While you are figuring out what that brand should be, sometimes it could be helpful to soak up knowledge by going to our invisible "undercover sister" mode where we can learn more by listening and observing others.

Depelsha McGruder—The Zigzag

Depelsha McGruder devised a specific strategy of climbing the ranks by working in a range of corporate functions. She would ask herself, "Does this job meet what I want to achieve?" She deliberately pursued various pieces of a corporate puzzle that would allow her to achieve her ultimate goal (as she wrote on her college application to Howard University) of "being a leader in communications and impacting the images African Americans see of themselves in the media."

- She went from being a reporter/storyteller at a local news station to Harvard Business School and transitioned to the management side of media.
- She spent time in consulting, a job she described as "a finishing school to business school." Next, she learned how to execute strategy, pitch ideas and navigate an organization by working in business development and strategy in a major media company.
- She moved then into operations. "I didn't want to stay in one vertical. I wanted to learn how to manage people as well as have profit–and–loss responsibilities. I wanted to know all of the building blocks of being a leader in media, so I could ultimately have real impact."

The major challenge she faced was explaining her career strategy to other people who take a more traditional path. One boss called her a "chameleon" because she had spent time in finance and marketing and programming as well as strategy. Depelsha concluded: "You have to have a story to tell about your choices. It's on me to connect the dots for people when pursuing an opportunity."

Two Routes to the Same Destination—Success

Some people are planners, while some are more spontaneous. Some follow zigzag paths, while others look for a straight line to the top. All of these strategies can work.

Bonita recommends that, as women of color, having a mental vision board or plan eases the process, a framework for what she calls "intentional perseverance."

You can always revisit your North Star and course correct your moves. Remember, careers are quite long. After completing business school, I decided I would take a path to the C–suite, which combined a skills–based approach and honing leadership principles. For my first decade, I set forth a vision to become a well-skilled marketer by following the four Ps of marketing–Pricing, Product, Place and Promotion. My first stop was hardware/software **Pricing,** *which at IBM resided in the financial planning department. I ascended quickly into my first line manager position as a financial manager. Upon realizing that this linear track was headed toward an accounting career, I took the call to head to the National Distribution Division and join the personal computer (PC) marketing team. At the time, we fondly referred to IBM as "I've been moved." I navigated myself smack in the middle of the PC heyday and the rise of personal computing, including the venerable DOS (Disk Operating System) developed by Microsoft for IBM in 1981. In the next decade, I practiced my entrepreneurial chops with two startups and then entered the automotive industry to learn scaled distribution* **(Place)** *and brand management and advertising* **(Promotion)**. *Having an understanding of the business power* *of technology, I joined Google to become a well–rounded digital executive across media, partnerships, emerging global markets and ad technology. As skills became strengths, I turned my attention to building a legacy of leadership. Throughout my career, I carried forth my favorite quote from Peter Drucker and the principles of innovation. He says, "The best way to predict the future is to create it." When in business doubt, create your way out. Create a new role, a new business, new ideas.*

Jackie followed a more spontaneous approach.

I observed HBS classmates who organized their lives with Excel spreadsheets. They had detailed monthly, yearly plans and executed them religiously. Instead, I used a less rigid approach. Like a duck gliding across a pond, I deliberately tried to appear to move effortlessly, serenely from assignment to assignment, success to success. No one else could see my feet paddling like mad just below the surface of the water.

I have always had an attitude of what I call "catching good." I would take every preparatory step I could. I would envision backup plans B, C and D, and then I would relax. I would open my spirit and look up with gratitude. Opportunities more exciting and fulfilling than any I might have prescribed on a spreadsheet always came my way. It was because I was open to them, looking up for them, instead of looking down, just grinding away. That's how covering presidential campaigns came my way as well as covering the White House.

When I moved to the Northeast Bureau in New York, I didn't have a particular affinity for covering the visual arts. One story came my way. I happened to enjoy the content and working with the producers who loved it as well. Together, we spent almost a decade reporting on blockbuster exhibits about the French impressionist painters and those who followed them (Monet, Renoir, Cezanne, Degas, Caillebotte, and also Sargent, Mary Cassatt, Miro, Matisse and Leger) as well as the most influential African American painters and sculptors of the 20th century (Jacob Lawrence, Elizabeth Catlett, William H. Johnson, Richard Hunt and the art collections of the historically Black colleges.)

My career was guided by a quote from futurist Robert Theobald. At a conference I helped organize as a college senior, Theobald said, "You will never be able to afford to retire. Therefore, make sure that your work is also your pleasure. That way, you will never resent having to work forever."

Even though the hours were long, and both the competition and the pressures were intense, I truly loved reporting and broadcasting. Until I didn't. At age 50, I relied upon my "insurance policy"–what I called my MBA earned at Harvard — to create a second career. Now, when people ask what I do, I echo that old Theobald quote and say, "Only what I want to do."

Leading from the Front...and from Behind

Nelson Mandela so aptly said, "It is better to lead from behind and to put others in front, especially when you celebrate victory when nice things occur. You take the front line when there is danger. Then people will appreciate your leadership."

If we update his quote for today, we should consider more angles. Know when to lead from the front. Sometimes, leading from the front entails recognizing and using the privileges that come with being the "first."

Leading from behind also is appropriate, especially when the work involves creativity and innovation. Again, quoting

Mandela, a shepherd "stays behind the flock, letting the nimblest go out ahead, whereupon the others follow, not realizing that all along they are being directed from behind."

HBS Professor Linda Hill used the Mandela quote in a famous *Harvard Business Review* article that articulated the major findings of her book, Collective Genius. People want to work in organizations that serve as positive forces in the world, she argued. And innovation comes when leaders build communities that can break through and create new approaches. After all, she wrote, "the shepherd makes sure that the flock stays together. He uses his staff to nudge and prod if the flock strays too far off course or into danger. For leaders, it's a matter of harnessing people's collective genius."[92]

Zuhairah Scott Washington - Leading from All Sides

Whether they lead from the front or from behind, the best senior executives, regardless of their industry, walk around their offices. It's a way of striking up random conversations, of learning what the troops are struggling with, of gathering needed "intel." And sometimes, it's a way of appearing–or genuinely being–empathetic.

People get caught up in titles. I say that you should lead where you are. You can grow and be cultivated no matter where you are in the organizational chart. Take the role you're in, and if you lead, you'll be given more responsibility. Markers of external or positional authority are fleeting and not substantive.

As a woman of color, it's a dance: When do you empower the team and when do you tell them what you want them to do?

189

I lead the way I want to be led. I very much want a team that feels empowered but also has clear guidance about what success looks like.

I'm not a totalitarian. I'm collaborative until things cross a line. I strive to ensure everyone on my team can make great decisions, whether I'm in the room or not. But I do drive to alignment if there are disagreements.

Seeding the Future—One Seed by One Seed

At every turn, both of us have sought to bust myths and stimulate progress. More recently, we have focused on helping the next generation.

Two years ago, Bonita was asked on an internal company panel what her legacy would be. The answer, she thought, could be found in a line that Lin–Manuel Miranda wrote for Alexander Hamilton: "What is a legacy? It's planting seeds in a garden you never get to see." A decade ago, her answer probably would have been similar to those of her colleagues, narrowly focused around current work goals. However, she took the question in a different direction and said her legacy would be "creating the next generation of leaders."

Bonita feels if you have earned the "privilege" of leadership, you should pass on your softer EQ (or emotional quotient) skills of coaching, team problem solving, addressing the more complicated people stuff, i.e. recruiting, hiring, performance management, firing and providing learning experience through untethered empowerment.

In 2017, Bonita was concerned the tech industry needed a more immersive approach to bolster African Americans in technology. She circulated the idea for a California campus among Google executives and Howard University President, Dr. Wayne Frederick. The idea was based on the premise that though HBCUs make up "just 3% of colleges and universities, they produce 27% of African American students with bachelor's degrees in STEM fields."[93] As a non–engineer, Bonita thought "what if" we create a "glass door" and bring select students to Silicon Valley for a more immersive experience. As a company, Google believes "ideas come from everywhere." Executives willingly rallied around the concept.

The program launched as "Howard West" and has since expanded to become the Google Tech Exchange program where more than 65 students from HBCUs and Hispanic Serving Institutions (HSI) participated in 2019, through courses co–taught by HBCU/HSI faculty and Google engineers. Bonita planted "a seed" for the "27%" and earned an A+ from her friends and relations for extending her own "privilege" to others by activating a longer term and more strategic vision.

Over the last decade or more, Jackie has often felt like an "old, rich white man" because she rubs shoulders with so many of them at the organizations she has frequented: the Council on Foreign Relations (CFR), the Chairman's Council of the New–York Historical Society, the Harvard Club of New York City, the HBS Club of New York, Juilliard's Evening Division and the United States Institute of Peace. She has made it her mission to ensure that she is not the last African American woman in those rooms.

To that end, she mentors numerous 20, 30 and even 40–somethings. Formally, she helps lead a successful training program for rising star managers of color in the media and in the marketing/communications divisions of Fortune 100 companies. The effort was launched with the support of the Ford Foundation and the Knight Foundation. Nearly 200 professionals have gone through the program in the last seven years. More than half were promoted or received raises within six months of participating, and many graduates have now assumed very senior roles in major news organizations.

Informally, she also supports the efforts of friends like Reta Jo Lewis, who has created the Women of Color in Transatlantic Leadership Forum, a growing group of Black and brown women in the military, the diplomatic corps and on Capitol Hill, who are "changing the face of foreign affairs."[94]

When You Think You've Lost and You've Won

We could merely lament the woes of women of color and particularly Black women. However, in writing this book, we have seen multiple examples of success, the results of unparalleled ambition. We see winners all around us–individually and collectively–but we believe that if we face that future together, there can be more, much more, for many. Think of that African proverb: "If you want to go quickly, go alone. If you want to go far, go together."

In our next and final chapter, we will explore our passion for teaming up and specific ways to do just that.

 **LIVING LOG**

❑ What/who would you include in a list of inspiring accomplishments by women of color?
❑ What are your favorite quotes about leadership?
❑ How do you define "leading while Black?" How is it different from leading individuals of various races?
❑ Do you shape your career with intentional perseverance or more randomly?
❑ How often do you express gratitude to yourself and others for what you've already won?
❑ What are your top five leadership tips?

Chapter Eight

Team Up!

Writing this book has been a journey of discovery for both of us, a true case study in teaming up. Before we began this project, we had admired each other's professional accomplishments from afar. We knew that each of us had been a unicorn, a pioneer, in our different realms, but we hadn't known many details about our actual experiences. We were astonished when we learned how much overlap there is in our families' histories and our middle–class childhoods.

- Both of us have knowledge of great grandfathers born into slavery who accumulated large landholdings after the Civil War (Bonita's in South Carolina and Jackie's in Louisiana); both men were described as "mulattos," meaning both were products of the rape culture of the time.
- Both of us have grandfathers who achieved multiple advanced degrees.
- Both of us were "Daddy's girls," and our fathers provided us with "force shields" for life.

- Both of our fathers passed away from heart disease at the same age of 47, while both of us were in college; Bonita was a freshman; Jackie was a senior.
- As we have written, in some respects, our achievements in business and the media were achievements for ourselves as well as for our fathers.
- And, finally, as we were completing this final chapter, we discovered our birthdays are in the same month, a few weeks apart.

Ours has been a perfect example of ideation meeting opportunity and opportunity meeting execution.

In her essay for Harvard Business School's commemoration of 50 years of women in the MBA program, Bonita issued a call to action: *"To all women of color, I say while we have been encouraged to 'Lean In,' we will do best if we TEAM UP. "*

When she shared her ideas for a book project and movement to help women of color thrive, Jackie was honored and awed. The unexpected and sudden threats to civil and women's rights in 2016 and 2017 had shocked her. Jackie wrote to Bonita: *"I realize that YOU are what I've been waiting for — a focus, a prompt, a partner to create something real and lasting, to give meaning to my adult experiences over the last half-century. Thank you!"*

Today, if you ask us, Bonita would say, *"I couldn't have written this book without Jackie's journalism skills and extensive network."* Jackie would say, *"People have been telling me to write a book for years, yet I couldn't have done it without Bonita's focus on something more important than the personal — as well as her entrepreneurial ability to organize information and collaborate effectively."*

Our partnership is powerful! Two minds really are better than one. Our symbiotic relationship echoes those in the natural world. One of our favorites is the story of mutual dependence between the ostrich and the zebra. While ostriches have poor senses of hearing and smell, zebras have bad eyesight. Ostriches and zebras often travel together to warn each other of possible dangers. They are crucial to each other's safety and survival.[95]

This analogy helps illustrate our central message about the context, requirements and benefits of women of color in business teaming up to lead, empower and thrive. We need each other. By teaming up, this project has become/ is becoming even better than we imagined when we started.

The Past Need Not Be Prologue

As we have explored subjects like stress and only–ness, the role of white male allies, mothers, fathers and finance, we have touched on elements of America's social, political, psychological and economic history. On its face, that history reflects what seems like a permanent tension between the brutality inflicted upon people of color and women — and the ideals upon which the United States was founded. That tension pits our moral conscience against our civic and economic realities.

Primarily, over the last half–century, until female historians and those of color began excavating and publicizing our stories, we have all been relegated to footnotes. For example, Harvard historian and celebrated author

Jill Lepore has observed there were only about 20,000 Pilgrims who immigrated across the Atlantic Ocean. Yet, some 15 million Africans were brought to North America against their will. She asks why one story has dominated our history books and the other, larger reality has been under–reported.

The revolution in Americans' understanding of the history of women and African slaves is occurring at the same time we confront new rounds of opposition to the goals of political and economic equality. People who have not been major participants in our national conversations are demanding to be heard and are seizing the tools to increase their effectiveness.

Change is indeed scary, but we are determined to do our part to make "sisters as a service" scalable to drive revenue inclusion in this country. If the economic power of women of color/entrepreneurs was fully activated, we could transform capitalism domestically and globally. While many businesses have focused on DEI (Diversity, Equity, Inclusion) with imperfect results, we see other businesses quietly harnessing the profitable factors associated with "revenue inclusion."

What's driving this change? We have pointed out several major trends in our earlier chapters:

- The college and graduate school graduation rates of women of color are skyrocketing.
- Likewise, the rates of entrepreneurship among women of color are higher than those of other groups, despite the near–total lack of outside venture capital.

- Women of color are continuing to rack up ground-breaking victories in fields as diverse as the military, ballet, politics and business. Assuming that demography is destiny, there should be a continuation of these wins.
- And our *Women of Color in Business: Cross Generational Survey©* confirmed the unparalleled ambition of Black women knowledge workers and our outsized confidence in the future.

The major question is how to accelerate and scale the progress of "sisters as a service," so that hopefully, someday soon, it will no longer be news when a woman of color is a "first" or an "only" or a unicorn—when our "blessing" is a given.

Techniques for Teaming Up—Lead, Empower and Thrive

While brainstorming strategies for delivering our "blessing," we have come up with a series of specific techniques. We have assembled them in three categories: lead, empower and thrive or LET.

I. LEAD

- Embrace the emerging leadership style that understands the exponential power of teams. And this includes all potential team engagement, whether it's your direct team, cross–functional team or relevant external teams. Collaborate or wither. Empower or stagnate.

- Over many decades of leadership, Bonita has experienced styles ranging from hierarchical, flat and the most effective of all: empowering others beyond yourself. As women leaders of color, we can create psychological safety because we know what it feels like to "feel safe." We know how to create an environment in which everyone can flourish. Release your authenticity as a "Wakanda" like power: absorb new ideas, give away credit without your ego invading the space and relish in the joy of empowering yourself and others to reach their full potential.

- The future belongs to high-performing teams. Bonita has led with this style, and her track record of leadership has been validated both inside and outside the organizations in which she has worked. When her HBS professor C. Roland Christensen, one of the founders of the field of business strategy, said she had "great potential," Bonita took the baton of her revered ally and ran. As we team up, always remember, batons are meant to be passed. Our goal: more women of color leaders at the top.

- Teaming up, sisters as a service, is happening across industries, within corporations and entrepreneurial ventures. The requirements are alliances, partnerships and honest feedback loops. We know that our youngest sisters are rating companies, both formally and informally through social media, about which are the best places for minorities to work.

- As several of our "chicks" have told us:

○ The next generation is not as patient as Boomers and Gen Xers were about leading. Millennials and Gen Zers are pushing. They're hungry, ambitious, not afraid to say, "This is my workplace and I need to thrive."

○ They're driving and pushing management to change. They operate with urgency. They're shaming companies that they work for."

• At Harvard Business School, some 700 women of color have been taught how to think, how to network, how to lead and how to give back. Up to now, we have all had our own personal successes. We have joined forces at various times in our various professional and social networks. But most of us have come together randomly. We have activated our referral networks in largely an ad hoc matter.

• What will it take to change that scenario? What will it take to scale our "sisters as a service" concept? We need to help each other, hire each other, learn from and support each other. We need to share information when we hear about corporate or major non–profit jobs and/or board openings. We need to recommend one another when we hear that award recipients are being selected. Our goal is to expand these opportunities–with and for our HBS colleagues — with and for so many others. Yes, ours is a disruptive idea, but isn't this the era of disruption? Let's seize it.

II. EMPOWER

• We must embrace generational sisterhood. Although birth mothers and daughters frequently have fraught relationships, partnerships between younger Gen Z and Millennial Black women and their older Boomer colleagues can be impactful. Just as, metaphorically, younger Black women (let's call them the ostriches) can see the future, we older Boomers (call us zebras) have experience and know the smell of predators. We older women have the battle scars and survival skills to help our younger daughters and sisters navigate their journeys. The young can help the older overcome the caution born of painful experiences.

- Our *Women of Color in Business: Cross Generational Survey©* makes the case. Our Gen Z Black (at 92%) and LatinX (at 90%) women are much more comfortable with the concept of "sisterhood" than their white counterparts (just 84%).

How important do you think "sisterhood" will be to you at work—in other words, other women, perhaps of the same race as you, who share good and bad times, exchange advice, and listen to each other's issues? (GenZ)

Black women	92%
LatinX women	90%
Asian women	83%
White women	84%

Women of Color in Business: Cross Generational Survey©

- Likewise, Black women overall say they are much more inclined to invent new solutions, to use their creativity; they are much less wedded to conventional wisdom than their white counterparts.

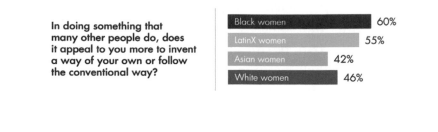

In doing something that many other people do, does it appeal to you more to invent a way of your own or follow the conventional way?

Black women — 60%
LatinX women — 55%
Asian women — 42%
White women — 46%

Women of Color in Business: Cross Generational Survey©

- And as marketers out there already know, our survey confirmed Black young women are first adopters; they are tech–forward; they are trendsetters.

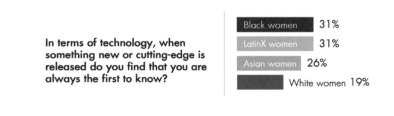

In terms of technology, when something new or cutting-edge is released do you find that you are always the first to know?

Black women — 31%
LatinX women — 31%
Asian women — 26%
White women 19%

Women of Color in Business: Cross Generational Survey©

- Our comfort with change and with sisterhood can and should be energized by our imminent demographic dominance. Black women and women of color will soon represent majorities in the United States. In some cities and states, we already are the majority. Using just sheer numbers, we need no longer be seen as the "under-represented in the underrepresented." Our impact is inevitable.

- This demographic, psycho–social movement, to us, reflects the "flywheel effect" described first some two decades ago by consultant and teacher Jim Collins in his famous book, *Good to Great*. Using Collins' analogy, the momentum of the sisters as a service movement is building and cannot be stopped.[96] To grow to its full potential, however, we participants must be doers, not complainers. We participants must be nimble to take advantage of myriad, unexpected benefits and avoid any missteps, as our proverbial flywheel grows bigger and bigger. Granted, our ambition may appear threatening to some, and there could be efforts to stop us, but the flywheel is already spinning. We are pulling people and opportunities toward us. This flywheel is improving ourselves and our economies, thereby ultimately driving wealth creation.

- There is no good reason for us to lower our eyes and shyly defer, deflect or fail to fulfill our potential. And we are willing to share with others.

- We have suggested our male allies would benefit if they adopted the posture of doormen and opened proverbial glass doors for women of color power-brokers. In some cases, these are places where very few of us have been but we—and more importantly YOU—know we belong because we represent the future of America.

- Those doors might include choosing us for promotions and raises, for new projects as well as stretch assignments. Another door could be providing honest feedback to us. We can take it. Yet another door might be asking our opinions, instead of assuming you know how we might react to any proposition. Rest assured. We are fully capable of opening our own glass doors! However, the trip will be much more pleasant with your collaboration.

III. THRIVE

- Machu Picchu, one of the new Seven Wonders of the World, offers the best lesson in trusting our natural grit. Located in the majestic Andes Mountains in Peru, this Inca treasure has many marvels, including its construction of more than 200 individual structures. When Bonita visited the site in 2016, she learned that when an earthquake occurs, the stones in an Inca building are said to "dance." They bounce through the tremors and then fall back into place. As businesswomen, we will have tremors along our career journeys. But just like the Peruvian marvels, we are the "miraculous" and we know how to dance; we know how to survive turbulent times. Hold steady, Ladies! [97]

- We do need to do a better job of hearing one another, of actively and empathetically listening to one another. Oppressors in the past have successfully pitted us against one another. We described the time–worn "divide and conquer" techniques earlier. But we know that game, and we now no longer have to play it. What we are saying here is that we need to treat other women of color with kindness and patience. We need to treat our sisters the way we would want to be treated, even if that means giving someone the benefit of the doubt. Know that there is psychological safety in the sister-hood and trust that our imaginations and ambitions can convey comfort within our unity.

- Our *Women of Color in Business: Cross Generational Survey*© found that very few of our 4,005 respondents are totally happy with the amount of wealth they have created to date. Our friend, Paula, told us that building wealth is increasingly a myth. Everyone, however, is looking for comfort, financial comfort. Jackie has found that comfort is redefining what "enough" income truly means and has adjusted her lifestyle accordingly. But we also have tips for assessing your personal appetite for risk and for prudently saving/investing to create financial comfort. Delayed gratification can deliver powerful results.

- In early 2019, we dined with Fortune & Forks, a group of recent college graduates who are teaming up to advance their individual career aspirations. They asked about our experiences in technology and the media, but we were struck by their questions about self–care. Bonita had useful advice about her decades–long dedi-cation to taking ballet classes. Jackie was dumbfound-ed. She had just soldiered on, endured stress–induced pathologies and didn't discover the benefits of exercise until her 40s.

  ○ We urge you to follow Bonita's path—not Jackie's. Take care of yourself. Find ways to reduce stress and live healthy lives. Flaming out early is not an option.

> A pedicure might not save the world, but it might just save your mental and physical health.

- And finally, repeating what we said in an earlier chapter: Let's blow away the poisonous fog of inferiority. It is a myth that oppressors have used to keep us down for centuries. **Just let it go.** It is just fog. It isn't real. What really matters at the end of the day is not our skin color or our reproductive organs. No one is inferior. Everyone is worthy. As Bonita's father advised so many years ago in his essay, "The Trail to Success," all that really matters is the content of our character, our courage and our ambition. The final line in his poem sums up the task:

In doing your noblest–"That's Success."

It's Up to Us

Scaling sisters as a service is happening, whether you participate or not. We urge you to participate! Zuhairah Scott Washington set the terms:

It's up to us! I have great confidence in us. There's probably no CEO of a Fortune 500 company who would say out loud that s/he doesn't care about or focus on diversity issues. But many DNI (diversity and inclusion) programs measure what I call "vanity metrics." These programs don't address the root causes of the lack of progress for senior leaders of color, and they don't really cultivate senior Black leaders, especially women.

That's why I say it's up to us. When I look at the careers of the handful of African American women senior executives, most of their careers have been self–made. They haven't risen through the regular institutional routes.

Our younger friends and colleagues concur and add a cautionary note:

Companies that want to be on the right side of history are championing DNI (diversity and inclusion). They not only want us to be successful, they NEED us to be successful, in positions of power and influence, because they understand that a failure to invest in us is a failure to invest in the future of this country.

Join Us

Researching our various chapters, we came across a variety of groups of women of color already teaming up. Some of the current efforts have noble, historical antecedents. For example:

- In professional tennis, Althea Gibson begat Venus and Serena Williams, who begat a whole crop of young stars, and they all support one another even as they compete.
- In politics, groundbreaking presidential candidate Congresswoman Shirley Chisholm begat The Squad–all the more meaningful in 2020, the centennial of the ratification of the 19th amendment to the Constitution giving women the right to vote.

This book may have reached its conclusion, but our journey hasn't. We are challenging you as we are challenging ourselves to deliver real, lasting change. Visit our website www.leadempowerthrive.com. Engage with our Living Log. Share the questions we raise and the techniques we list with your teams.

Even in the face of external economic and public health challenges, we can create a productive, prosperous future for all of our sisters — together.

Acknowledgments

Practicing gratitude is one of the techniques that we suggest, and this is the place in our book where we have the opportunity to express it.

Conceptualizing our themes and launching our partnership grew out of mutual admiration and avocado toast, but each of us brought a lifetime of experiences and connections to this effort. If we have overlooked anyone, we have done so inadvertently.

First, we would like to thank our friend, first reader and chief disrupter, our publisher, Marva Allen. She saw the potential in our story. She drove us to pursue fresh, bold and fierce thinking. She urged us to share a little told story, that of the Black middle class.

We would also like to thank Sumya Ojakli, who saw the potential for our ideas becoming more than just a book.

We owe huge debts of gratitude to our polling guru, Scott Siff, and his talented staff at Quadrant Strategies. Chief among them are Hannah Leverson and Mary Amis.

We want to thank the Harvard Business School colleagues who contributed to our manuscript: Dr. Modupe Akinola (MBA 2001, PhD 2009), Beverly Anderson (MBA 1997),

Janelle Faulk (PLDA 27), Kimberly Foster (MBA 2020), Amanda E. Johnson (MBA 2014), Depelsha McGruder (MBA 1998), Denise Murrell (MBA 1980), Zuhairah Scott Washington (JD/MBA 2005) and Michelle Morris Weston (MBA 1983).

In addition, we are grateful to have benefited from the extended wisdom of current and former HBS professors: James Cash, Robin Ely, Linda Hill, Henry McGee, Anthony Mayo, Tsedal Neeley, Laura Morgan Roberts, Steven Rogers and David Thomas.

As you can tell, we both are deeply involved in the HBS community and a number of alums provided inspiration: Ann Fudge, Nancy Lane, Kenneth Powell, Lillian Lincoln Lambert, Dame Vivian Hunt, Ivy Jack, Keith Butler, Craig Robinson, Karen Brown, Jacqueline Jones, Mark and Lisa Skeete Tatum, Grace Chao, Mary Jo Veverka, Catherine Flynn, Sheila Talton and Jacqueline Burgos.

We want to thank our Fortune & Forks hosts, Krystal Vega and Naomi Wright.

Jackie is indebted to Mark Carter and a talented group of rising star managers of color in media, tech and finance who helped us appreciate and articulate the concept of generational diversity: Joey Cole, Adrien Hopkins, Koshie Nartley, Muna Mushien, Wesley Oliver and the incomparable Sumorwuo Zaza. Spelman alums Alexis Crews and Melissa Grant also contributed in this area.

Bonita specifically wants to thank:

My lifelong team that consistently stimulated my curiosity and ability to think beyond myself to always ask "What if."

My sisterhood: Cheryl Mayberry McKissack, for her entrepreneurial spirit, inspiration and for being the sister I always wanted and my partner for two companies, One Moment in Time and NiaOnline.

Star Jones and the Brown Girls: (you know who you are).

My close confidantes for bringing this vision to reality: Gina Stikes, Janki Darity, Priscilla Brown, Suzanne Shank Werdlow, Sharon Deberry, Shirley Moulton and Asmau Admed.

My business village: Google for giving me a place to tinker in my sandbox of ideas and become part of a broader mission. And every single team I've ever led: "The Bat Cave," "FEAT" and LPS. You shaped me as a leader.

My alliances: Harvard Business School African–American Alumni Association, Black Googler Network, Women@ Google, Google Black Leadership Advisory Group, Women@ Partnerships, Women's Forum, Chief, Executive Leadership Council.

My sacred space. Ballet Academy East, Classic Ballet Academy, American Ballet Theatre.

My trusted allies and sponsors who graciously lent their support, encouragement and made a bet on me: Cappy Black, Bill McCracken, Marty Levine, Jim Schroer, Tim Armstrong, Jeff Levick, Dennis Woodside, Nikesh Arora, Margo Georgiadis, Philipp Schlinder, Don Harrison, Scott Sheffer and Torrence Boone.

My devoted and loving parents John, and Margaret Coleman, who left too soon, yet left an indelible mark on my soul, my brothers Gerald Coleman and John Coleman III who were the tailwind for my dreams, my

Gen Z niece, Gabrielle Coleman (who pushed for the original title–*A Blessing*) and my mother's best friend, Mrs. Mildred Smith who has provided a watchful eye over my well–being.

My most memorable educators: Third–grade teacher Mrs. Thomas, Howard University Professor Samuel Yette and HBS Professor Roland Christensen.

My loving husband who supported me as I juggled a book, a full–time job, my corporate board work and home life.

Jackie specifically wants to thank:

Those friends and colleagues from CBS News, my consulting career and my various non–profit activities who provided invaluable insights, recollections, recommendations and reinforcement: Brian Healy, Alvin Hall, Linda Richardson, Marlys Appleton, Calvin Sims and Patricia Baptiste, Arlene and Chester Salomon, Ursula Day, Jennifer Siebens, Marsha Cooke, Terry and Bill Whitaker, Bill Plante and Robin Smith, Michelle Miller, Ambassador Roman Popadiuk, Reta Jo Lewis, Randall Tucker and Raymond Vessey, Marco Greenberg, Libby Schnee, Dr. Marisa Tramontano, Harriet Friedlander, Peter and Joanne Ackerman, Karen Toulon, Tom and Sheila Buckmaster, Susan Hakarrainen, Melissa Andresko, Michelle Gadsden–Williams, Laura Washington, Pam Schafler, Judith Batty, Tina Walls, Paula Rivera, Gwen Adams Norton, Juilliard Evening Division Professor Reggie Quinerly as well as the leaders and students of the KIPP Charter Schools in New York City and our HBSAAA volunteers.

My extraordinarily dear family by choice (you know who you are).

Jointly, we want to thank leaders everywhere who take seriously their responsibility for activating the intellectual power of the collective, our teams of promising women of color.

As we close this last section of our writing and open a world of opportunity for a new meaning of togetherness, let's imagine a new world. We are standing before our ancestors, those strong, indomitable, courageous individuals to whom we dedicated this book, our ancestors who were brought to this land against their will, in chains. We hear them asking a soul–wrenching question: "What did you do for our people when you were free?"

This book and this platform are down payments on that answer.

Endnotes Index

A Note from the Authors

1. Methodology for *Women of Color in Business: Cross Generational Survey©*: This study was commissioned by the authors of this book and conducted by Quadrant Strategies. Quadrant surveyed 4,005 desk workers, who identified as women, including 1,604 African American women, 1,600 Latinx women, 403 Asian women, and 401 white women. Respondents were surveyed from October to November 2019. With a 95% confidence interval, the margin of error for African American women and Latinx women is ±2.45%; the margin of error for Asian women is ±4.88%; and the margin of error for white women is ±4.89%.   *page 2*

Introduction

2. Divide and Rule definition.
   𝒫 https://en.wikipedia.org/wiki/Divide_and_rule   *page 8*

3. Blow, Charles W., "White Extinction Anxiety." *The New York Times.* June 6, 2018
   𝒫 https://www.nytimes.com/2018/06/24/opinion/america-white -extinction.html   *page 12*

4. Pace, Cindy, "How Women of Color Get to Senior Management" *Harvard Business Review.* August 31, 2018
   𝒫 https://hbr.org/2018/08/how-women-of-color-get-to-senior -management   *page 13*

5. Marshall, Melinda and Wingfield, Tai, "Getting More Black Women into the C-Suite." *Harvard Business Review.* July 1, 2016
   𝒫 https://hbr.org/2016/07/getting-more-black-women-into-the -c-suite   *page 14*

6. Hinchliffe, Emma, "The number of female CEOs in the Fortune 500 hits an all-time record." *Fortune.* May 18, 2020
   𝒫 https://bit.ly/2XHBs2w   *page 14*

7. McKinsey & Co. and Lean In.org, "Women in the Workplace 2018 and 2019"
  𝒫 https:// womenintheworkplace.com/   *page* 15

8. Busch, William F. and Tapia, Andres, "Why African American talent is opting out." Korn Ferry.
  𝒫 https://www.kornferry.com/insights/articles/perspective-african -american-talent   *page* 15

9. "The 2018 State of Women-Owned Businesses Report," commissioned by American Express.
  𝒫 https://about.americanexpress.com/files/doc_library/file/2018-state -of-women-owned-businesses-report.pdf   *page* 16

10. "Rapidly rising: Business ownership surging for black women as challenges remain." *TEN,* the magazine of the Federal Reserve Bank of Kansas City. November 8, 2018
  𝒫 https://kansascityfed.org/en/publications/ten/articles/2018/ fall2018/rapidly-rising   *page* 16

11. The Harvard Business School African-American Alumni Association Profiles.
  𝒫 http://www.hbsaaa.net/   *page* 17

12. Caldwell, Arthur Bunyan. "History of the American Negro-South Carolina edition." A.B. Publishing Company. 1919 copyright   *page* 18

13. Roberts, Laura Morgan, Mayo, Anthony J., Thomas, & David A. *Race, Work, and Leadership: New Perspectives on the Black Experience,* Harvard Business Review Press, 2019.   *page* 19

14. Houston, Pam. "The Truest Eye." *O, The Oprah Magazine,* November 2003.
  𝒫 https://www.oprah.com/omagazine/toni-morrison-talks-love/all *page* 19

Chapter One—Our Natural Grit

15. Roberts, Laura Morgan, Mayo, Anthony J., Thomas, & David A., editors. *Race, Work, and Leadership: New Perspectives on the Black Experience,* Harvard Business Review Press, 2019.   *page* 22

16. Halliday, Jean, "Interactive Marketer of the Year: Chrysler" Ad Age." *Ad Age.* November 7, 2005
  𝒫 https://adage.com/article/special-report-creative-marketers/interac-tive-marketer-year-chrysler/105108   *page* 23

17. Warrell, Margie, "How Women Can Take the Lead in Levelling the Playing Field." *Forbes.* July 20, 2019
  𝒫 https://bit.ly/2XSLE8w   *page* 24

18. Riggio, Ronald E., PhD. "Why Women Make Better Leaders than Men." *Psychology Today.* March 9, 2010
🔗 https://www.psychologytoday.com/us/blog/cutting-edge-leadership/201003/why-women-make-better-leaders-men *page 24*

19. Marshall, Melinda and Wingfield, Tai, "Getting More Black Women into the C-Suite." *Harvard Business Review.* July 1, 2016
🔗 https://hbr.org/2016/07/getting-more-black-women-into-the-c-suite *page 25*

20. The African American Population. *Black Demographics.* The American Community Survey of the U.S. Census Bureau.
🔗 https://blackdemographics.com/population/black-women-statistics/ *page 26*

21. McKinsey & Co. and Lean In.org, "Women in the Workplace 2018 and 2019."
🔗 https:// womenintheworkplace.com/ *page 26*

22. Duckworth, Angela, "Grit: The Power of Passion and Perseverance." Scribner. 2016 *page 26*

23. Knowledge is Power Program, Character Education.
🔗 https://www.kippendeavor.org/character-education *page 27*

24. Greene, David. Author Interviews: "'Children Succeed' With Character Not Test Scores." Heard on *Morning Edition.* NPR. September 4, 2012
🔗 https://www.npr.org/2012/09/04/160258240/children-succeed-with-character-not-test-scores *page 28*

25. *Obituary and Family tree prepared by Ronald Coleman* and Caldwell, Arthur Bunyan. "History of the American Negro-South Carolina edition." A.B. Publishing Company. 1919 copyright *page 29*

26. Leave it to Beaver definition.
🔗 https://en.wikipedia.org/wiki/Leave_It_to_Beaver *page 29*

27. "1948 — Integrating the Air Force." Air Force Historical Support Division. Published April 6, 2011
🔗 https://www.afhistory.af.mil/FAQs/Fact-Sheets/Article/458996/1948-integrating-the-air-force/ *page 36*

Chapter Two—The Power of Value

28. Heilman, M.E. & Parks-Stamm, E.J. (2007). Gender stereotypes in the workplace: Obstacles to women's career progress. In S.J. Correll (Ed.), Social Psychology of Gender. Advances in Group Processes (Volume 24) 47-78. Elsevier Ltd., JAI Press.
🔗 http://as.nyu.edu/content/nyu-as/as/faculty/madeline-e-heilman.html *page 45*

29. Howard, Jacqueline. "New Study Confirms Depressing Truth about Names and Racial Bias." *Huffington Post.* October 8, 2015 🔗 https://www.huffpost.com/entry/black-sounding-names-study_n _561697a5e4b0dbb8000d687f *page 46*

30. Deyle, Steven. "Carry Me Back: The Domestic Slave Trade in American Life." Oxford University Press. 2006 *page 49*

31. Beckert, Sven and Rockman, Seth, editors. "Slavery's Capitalism A New History of American Economic Development." Penn Press. 2016 *page 49*

32. McGruder, Depelsha. Facebook post, December 12, 2019. 🔗 https://www.facebook.com/depelsha.mcgruder/posts/ 10213444824109928 *page 49*

33. Adams, Kimberly. "The disturbing parallels between modern accounting and the business of slavery" "Marketplace," *Minnesota Public Radio.* August 14, 2018 🔗 https://bit.ly/3eFin8g *page 50*

34. Gates, Jr., Henry Louis. "Frederick Douglass's Camera Obscura," *Aperture Magazine,* Summer 2016 *page 50*

35. Meier, Allison. "Library of Congress Digitizes 19th-Century Photos of Black Women Activists," *Hyperallergic.com.* April 6, 2017 🔗 https://hyperallergic.com/370345/19th-century-photographs-of -black-women-activists/ *page 51*

36. McGirt, Ellen. "raceAhead: A New Nielsen Report Puts Black Buying Power at $1.2 Trillion," *Fortune.* February 28, 2018 🔗 https://fortune.com/2018/02/28/raceahead-nielsen-report-black -buying-power/ *page 51*

37. McGirt, Ellen. "raceAhead: Black Women Company Founders Need Investment," *Fortune.* June 13, 2018 🔗 https://bit.ly/2TXVYLc *page 58*

38. Noel, Nick, Pinder, Duwain, Stewart III, Shelley and Wright, Jason. "The Economic Impact of Closing the Racial Wealth Gap." McKinsey & Company. August 13, 2019 🔗 https://www.mckinsey.com/industries/public-sector/our-insights/ the-economic-impact-of-closing-the-racial-wealth-gap *page 58*

Chapter Three—Onward Sole Sisters

39. The African American Population. *Black Demographics.* The American Community Survey of the U.S. Census Bureau. 🔗 https://blackdemographics.com/population/black-women-statistics/ *page 76*

40. Milano, Brett. "How slavery still shadows healthcare." *The Harvard Gazette*. October 29, 2019
   🔗 https://bit.ly/2At1xe1   *page 77*

41. Rabin, Roni Caryn. "Hair Dyes and Straighteners May Raise Breast Cancer Risk for Black Women." *The New York Times*. December 4, 2019.
   🔗 https://www.nytimes.com/2019/12/04/health/cancer-hair-dye -black-women.html   *page 79*

42. Krivkovich, Alexis, Nadeau, Marie-Claude, Robinson, Kelsey, Robinson, Nicole, Starikova, Irina and Yee, Lareina. "Women in the Workplace, 2018," McKinsey & Company. October 23, 2018.
   🔗 https://www.mckinsey.com/featured-insights/gender-equality/ women-in-the-workplace-2018   *page 80*

43. Roberts, Laura Morgan, Mayo, Anthony J., Thomas, & David A. *Race, Work, and Leadership: New Perspectives on the Black Experience*, Harvard Business Review Press, 2019.   *page 81*

44. Network of Executive Women News online.
   🔗 https://www.newonline.org/news-insights/news/catalyst-report -bias-unhealthy-women-color   *page 82*

45. The Harvard Business School African-American Alumni Association Profiles.
   🔗 http://www.hbsaaa.net/zuhairah-washington.php   *page 82*

46. Yang, Jessica. "For Women of Color in Medicine, the Challenges Extend Beyond Education," *Zora/Medium.com*. September 9, 2019.
   🔗 https://zora.medium.com/for-women-of-color-in-medicine-the -challenges-extend-beyond-education-4df4e4b78b58   *page 85*

47. Wilkins, David B. and Fong, Bryan. *Intersectionality and the Careers of Black Women Lawyers* in Roberts, Laura Morgan, Mayo, Anthony J., Thomas, & David A., editors. *Race, Work, and Leadership: New Perspectives on the Black Experience*, Harvard Business Review Press, 2019.   *page 86*

48. Smothers, Hannah. "All 19 Black Women Running for Judge in a Texas Race Won Tuesday Night," *Cosmopolitan*. November 7, 2018
   🔗 https://www.cosmopolitan.com/politics/a24787624/black-women -harris-county-judicial-race-midterms-2018   *page 87*

49. Peoples, Lindsay. "Why the Election of 9 Black Female Judges in Alabama Matters," *The Cut, New York Magazine*. January 20, 2017
   🔗 https://www.thecut.com/2017/01/why-the-election-of-9-black -female-judges-in-alabama-matters.html   *page 87*

50. Kingkade, Tyler. "Students Of Color Aren't Getting The Mental Health Help They Need In College," *HuffPost.com*. February 2, 2017 *&* https://www.huffpost.com/entry/students-of-color-mental-health _n_5697caa6e4b0ce49642373b1   *page 90*

51. Dockterman, Eliana. "Under Armour's Stunning Ballerina Ad Aims to Lure Women From Lululemon," *Time*. August 5, 2014 *&* https://time.com/3083114/misty-copeland-under-armour-i-will -what-i-want/   *page 91*

52. Pauley, Jane. "Faces of Depression: Terrie Williams," *Take One Step: Caring for Depression, PBS* 2008 *&* https://www.pbs.org/wgbh/takeonestep/depression/ faces-terrie.html   *page 93*

53. McIntosh, Peggy. Excerpted from Working Paper 189. "White Privilege and Male Privilege: A Personal Account of Coming To See Correspondences through Work in Women's Studies, (1988)," *Independent School*. Winter 1990 *&* https://www.racialequitytools.org/resourcefiles/mcintosh.pdf *page 99*

54. Frazier, Ian. "When W. E. B. Du Bois Made a Laughingstock of a White Supremacist," *The New Yorker*. August 19, 2019 *&* https://www.newyorker.com/magazine/2019/08/26/when-w-e -b-du-bois-made-a-laughingstock-of-a-white-supremacist   *page 102*

55. Peck, M. Scott, MD, "The Road Less Traveled," Touchstone. 2003   *page 106*

Chapter Four—Never Give Up!

56. Stallings, Erika. "If You're a Young Black Woman in Corporate America, You're More Likely to Be Underpaid — And Stressed," *O, The Oprah Magazine*. August 20, 2019 *&* https://www.oprahmag.com/life/work-money/a28569015/black -women-underpaid-stress/   *page 110*

57. Herrera, Tim. "How Early-Career Setbacks Can Set You Up for Success," *The New York Times*. October 29, 2019 *&* https://www.nytimes.com/2019/10/27/smarter-living/career -advice-overcome-setback.html?searchResultPosition=3   *page 115*

58. Dalio, Ray. "Principles: Life and Work," Simon & Schuster. 2017   *page 118*

59. Onibada, Ade. "Here's Why Black British Women Find Michelle Obama's Story Way Too Relatable," www.buzzfeed.com. December 6, 2018 *&* https://www.buzzfeed.com/adeonibada/british-black-women- michelle-obamas-becoming-story

60. Smith, Melissa. "How A Businesswoman Became A Voice for Art's Black Models," *The New York Times*. December 26, 2018 🔗 https://www.nytimes.com/2018/12/26/arts/design/posing -modernity-curator-manet-olympia.html *page 124*

61. Hill, Lincoln. "Why the Imposter Syndrome is Worse for Women of Color," *Zora.medium.com*. July 25, 2019 🔗 https://zora.medium.com/why-imposter-syndrome-is-worse-for -women-of-color-3bcf37335405 *page 125*

62. Nunez, Vivian. "Ellen Ochoa Was The First Latina To Go To Space, Now She Shares Her Top Career Lessons," *Forbes.com*. September 23, 2019 🔗 https://bit.ly/2ZREu7g *page 127*

63. McGregor, Jena. "Lawmakers to introduce first federal bills to ban race -based hair discrimination," *The Washington Post*. December 5, 2019 🔗 https://www.washingtonpost.com/business/2019/12/05/lawmakers -introduce-first-federal-bills-ban-race-based-hair-discrimination/ *page 129*

64. Adams, Char. "Why We Need More Black Women Workspaces," *Zora.medium.com*. August 15, 2019 🔗 https://zora.medium.com/why-we-need-more-black-women -workspaces-90f89b908001 *page 129*

Chapter Five—Dreaming of Allies

65. McKinsey & Company. "Women in the Workplace 2018" 🔗 https://womenintheworkplace.com/ *page 132*

66. Washington, Zuhairah and Roberts, Laura Morgan. "Women of Color Get Less Support at Work. Here's How Managers Can Change That." *Harvard Business Review*. March 4, 2019 🔗 https://hbr.org/2019/03/women-of-color-get-less-support-at-work -heres-how-managers-can-change-that *page 133*

67. Ford, Ashley C. "Serena Williams: The Power of Unapologetic Greatness," *Allure Magazine*. January 10, 2019. 🔗 https://bit.ly/3clzZV1 *page 133*

68. Johnson, Stephanie K. and Hekman, David R. "Women and Minorities Are Penalized for Promoting Diversity," *Harvard Business Review*. March 23, 2016 quoted in Roberts, Laura Morgan, Mayo, Anthony J., Thomas, & David A., editors. *Race, Work, and Leadership: New Perspectives on the Black Experience*, Harvard Business Review Press, 2019. *page 133*

69. Williams, Joan C. "How Women Can Escape the Likeability Trap," *The New York Times*. August 16, 2019 🔗 https://www.nytimes.com/2019/08/16/opinion/sunday/gender -bias-work.html *page 134*

70. Roberts, Laura Morgan, Mayo, Anthony J., Thomas, & David A., editors. *Race, Work, and Leadership: New Perspectives on the Black Experience,* Harvard Business Review Press, 2019. *page 134*

71. Harding, Xavier. "Coding Diversity into Silicon Valley," *Popular Science.* August 29, 2019
🔗 https://www.popsci.com/black-girls-code-kimberly-bryant-coding-diversity-into-silicon-valley/ *page 137*

72. Greenfield, Rebecca. "The White-Male Mentorship Premium," *Bloomberg.* August 9, 2019
https://www.bloomberg.com/news/articles/2019-08-09/white-male-mentorship-brings-a-premium-and-it-s-hurting-women *page 139*

73. Bourke, Juliet and Dillon, Bernadette. "6 Characteristics of Inclusive Leaders," *The Wall Street Journal.* December 13, 2016
🔗 https://deloitte.wsj.com/cmo/2016/12/13/6-characteristics-of-inclusive-leaders/ *page 141*

74. "Automobile Industry Avoids Employing Jews in Administrative Posts," *Jewish Telegrahic Agency.* October 7, 1963
🔗 https://www.jta.org/1963/10/07/archive/automobile-industry-avoids-employing-jews-in-administrative-posts *page 143*

75. The Harvard Business School African-American Alumni Association Profiles. www.hbsaaa.net *page 149*

76. Auger-Dominguez, Daisy. "Getting Over Your Fear of Talking About Diversity." *Harvard Business Review.* November 08, 2019
https://hbr.org/2019/11/getting-over-your-fear-of-talking-about-diversity *page 151*

77. Washington, Zuhairah and Roberts, Laura Morgan. "Women of Color Get Less Support at Work. Here's How Managers Can Change That." *Harvard Business Review.* March 4, 2019
🔗 https://hbr.org/2019/03/women-of-color-get-less-support-at-work-heres-how-managers-can-change-that *page 151*

Chapter Six—Women@Work+

78. Omeokwe, Amara. "Women Overtake Men as Majority of U.S. Workforce," *The Wall Street Journal.* January 10, 2020
🔗 https://www.wsj.com/articles/women-overtake-men-as-majority-of-u-s-workforce-11578670615?mod=djemalertNEWS *page 157*

79. "Breadwinner Mothers by Race/Ethnicity and State," Institute for Women's Policy Research, Quick Figures. September 2016.
🔗 https://iwpr.org/wp-content/uploads/wpallimport/files/iwpr-export/publications/Q054.pdf *page 158*

80. Ely, Robin, Stone, Pamela, Shannon, Laurie and Ammerman, Colleen. Harvard Business School Spheres of Influence Alumni Survey, "Life & Leadership After HBS." May 2015.
  ℗ https://www.hbs.edu/women50/docs/L_and_L_Survey_2Findings _13final.pdf *page* 158

81. Slaughter, Ann-Marie. "How Older Women Are Trying to Change the World," *Financial Times*. November 7, 2019
  ℗ https://www.ft.com/content/bd811d5c-f96c-11e9-a354-36acbbb0d9b6 *page* 169

Chapter Seven—Winning

82. Okahan, H. and Zhou, E. "Graduate Enrollment and Degrees: 2006 to 2016," Council of Graduate Schools, 2017; *Spheres of Influence: A Portrait of Black MBA program alumni*, HBS, April 2018. *page* 172

83. Marco, Tony. "West Point is about to Graduate its Largest Class of Black Women," *CNN*. May 27, 2019
  ℗ https://www.cnn.com/2019/05/15/us/west-point-largest -graduating-class-of-black-women-trnd/index.html *page* 174

84. Zaveri, Mihir. "Miss America, Miss Teen USA and Miss USA Are All Black Women for the First Time," *The New York Times*. May 5, 2019
  ℗ https://www.nytimes.com/2019/05/05/style/miss-teen-usa-america -black.html *page* 174

85. Vulpo, Mike. "Why Zozibini Tunzi's Miss Universe 2019 Win Is Especially Historic," *E News*. December 9, 2019
  ℗ https://www.eonline.com/au/news/1100890/why-zozibini-tunzi-s -miss-universe-2019-win-is-especially-historic *page* 174

86. Armour, Nancy. "Gymnastics championships: Simone Biles penalized for being too good," *USA Today*. October 5, 2019
  ℗ https://bit.ly/3coHZEE *page* 174

87. Kourlas, Gia. "After Misty Comes Marie: Breaking Barriers in 'The Nutcracker'," *The New York Times*. November 28, 2019
  ℗ https://www.nytimes.com/2019/11/28/arts/dance/ nutcracker-Marie.html *page* 175

88. Lee, Taeku and Lee, EunSook. "Why Trump Fears Women of Color," *The New York Times*. August 13, 2019
  ℗ https://www.nytimes.com/2019/08/13/opinion/trump-black -women-2020.html?action=click&module=Opinion&pgtype=Homepag *page* 176

89. Shetterly, Margot Lee. 26 Women of Color Diversifying Entrepreneurship in Silicon Valley, Media, and Beyond," *Vanity Fair*, April 2018 𝒫 https://www.vanityfair.com/news/2018/03/women-of-color -diversifying-entrepreneurship-in-silicon-valley-media-and-beyond *page* 177

90. Hannon, Kerry. "Starting Your Own Business Is Hard. Here's Some Advice," *The New York Times*. November 19, 2019 𝒫 https://www.nytimes.com/2019/11/19/business/women -entrepreneurs-advice.html *page* 177

91. Roberts, Laura Morgan, Mayo, Anthony J., Thomas, & David A., editors. *Race, Work, and Leadership: New Perspectives on the Black Experience,* Harvard Business Review Press, 2019. *page* 182

92. Hill, Linda A. "Leading from Behind," *Harvard Business Review*. May 5, 2010 𝒫 https://hbr.org/2010/05/leading-from-behind *page* 189

93. White House Initiative on Educational Excellence for African Americans. U.S. Department of Education, "Fact Sheet: Spurring African-American STEM Degree Completion." March 16, 2016 𝒫 https://www.ed.gov/news/press-releases/fact-sheet-spurring -african-american-stem-degree-completion *page* 191

94. The German Marshall Fund of the United States. "The Third Annual Women of Color in Transatlantic Leadership Forum: Changing the Face of Foreign Affairs," December 6, 2019 𝒫 https://www.gmfus.org/events/third-annual-women-color -transatlantic-leadership-forum-changing-face-foreign-affairs *page* 192

Chapter Eight—Team Up

95. Symbiotic relationships: Zebra and Ostrich. 𝒫 https://animalsymbiosis.weebly.com/zebra-and-ostrich.html *page* 196

96. Collins, Jim C. "Good to Great: Why Some Companies Make the Leap.... and Others Don't," William Collins, 2001. *page* 203

97. Adams, Mark. "Discover 10 secrets of Machu Picchu," *National Geographic*. November 6, 2018 𝒫 https://www.nationalgeographic.com/travel/top-10/peru/machu -picchu/secrets/ *page* 204

Resources

Moms of Black Boys United For Change — https://www.mobbunited.org/

Calculate My Wealth — http://calculatemywealth.com/wealth-calculator/

Interviews with HBS alumnae contributors and others

Dr. Modupe Akinola (MBA 2001, PhD 2009) — January 26, 2019

Beverly Anderson (MBA 1997) — February 1, 2019

Janelle Faulk (PLDA 27) — December 1, 2019

Kimberly Foster (MBA 2020) — November 23, 2019

Amanda E. Johnson (MBA 2014) — December 23, 2019

Depelsha McGruder (MBA 1998) — December 9, 2019

Denise Murrell (MBA 1980) — December 14, 2019

Zuhairah Scott Washington (JD/MBA 2005) — October 19 and December 18, 2019

Michelle Morris Weston (MBA 1983) — January 9, 2020

"Paula" — October 9, 2019

Brian Healy — November 27, 2018

Sumorwuo Zaza — November 22, 2019

Focus group of alumni of The Diverse Future — December 1, 2019

Fortune & Forks participants — January 15, 2019

Spelman alums Alexis Crews and Melissa Grant — October 21, 2018